"This book is the eloquent story of one mother's efforts to find her way after the death of her son by suicide, from raw numbness to slow sense-making. Unlike most suicide loss survivor narratives, it is helpfully organized around themes and issues that survivors will inevitably encounter, such as the bodily impact of suicide loss and guilt and responsibility. Who should read this book? Anyone who has lost a loved one to suicide; any parent who has lost a child (to any cause); anyone who wishes to support a suicide loss survivor; and above all, any and every mother who has lost a child to suicide. It will help you navigate your own painful journey towards peace."

—*John R. Jordan, Ph.D., Psychologist, trainer, international authority on suicide loss, and co-author of* Grief After Suicide: Understanding the Consequences and Caring for the Survivors

"Auerbach's intimate, heart-wrenching story of a mother's grief normalizes the grief experience for other suicide loss survivors and creates awareness regarding complicated grief after sudden death. As you read and experience the searing pain, you are led in the end to the promise of renewal—and to a celebration of life."

—*Iris Bolton, author of* My Son, My Son: A Guide to Healing After Death, Loss or Suicide, *founder of survivor support group movement, and Director Emeritus, The Link Counseling Center and the National Resource Center for Suicide Prevention & Aftercare*

"What is so special about Auerbach's moving memoir about the suicide of her remarkable son Noah is how he comes across so alive and present. Auerbach is searingly honest, and her observations and practical advice offer hope and comfort to others who are on their own personal journeys of mourning the suicide of their loved ones, especially those with recent loss."

—*Carla Fine, author of* No Time to Say Goodbye: Surviving the Suicide of a Loved One

"Auerbach faces down her demons after her father's suicide (when she was 26) and her 21-year-old son Noah's suicide (three years ago) to offer survivors this wide-ranging set of extremely helpful tools—conventional therapeutic aids, journaling, faith, yoga and meditation exercises, and thoughtful introspection—for better coping and healing after suicide loss."

—*William Feigelman, Ph.D. co-author of* Devastating Losses: How Parents Cope with the Loss of a Child to Suicide or Drugs

I'll Write Your Name on Every Beach

of related interest

After the Suicide
Helping the Bereaved to Find a Path from Grief to Recovery
Kari Dyregrov, Einar Plyhn and Gudrun Dieserud
ISBN 978 1 84905 211 5
eISBN 978 0 85700 445 1

Love after Death
Bereaved Parents and their Continuing Bonds
Catherine Seigal
ISBN 978 1 78592 326 5
eISBN 978 1 78450 641 4

We Get It
Voices of Grieving College Students and Young Adults
Heather L. Servaty-Seib and David C. Fajgenbaum
ISBN 978 1 84905 752 3
eISBN 978 0 85700 977 7

Supporting People through Loss and Grief
An Introduction for Counsellors and Other Caring Practitioners
John Wilson
ISBN 978 1 84905 376 1
eISBN 978 0 85700 739 1

The Essential Guide to Life after Bereavement
Beyond Tomorrow
Judy Carole Kauffmann and Mary Jordan
ISBN 978 1 84905 335 8
eISBN 978 0 85700 669 1

I'll Write Your Name on Every Beach

A MOTHER'S QUEST FOR COMFORT, COURAGE, AND CLARITY AFTER SUICIDE LOSS

Susan Averbach

Jessica Kingsley *Publishers*
London and Philadelphia

For permissions see page 215

First published in 2017
by Jessica Kingsley Publishers
73 Collier Street
London N1 9BE, UK
and
400 Market Street, Suite 400
Philadelphia, PA 19106, USA

www.jkp.com

Copyright © Susan Auerbach 2017

Front cover image source: Susan Auerbach

Library of Congress Cataloging in Publication Data
A CIP catalog record for this book is available from the Library of Congress

British Library Cataloguing in Publication Data
A CIP catalogue record for this book is available from the British Library

ISBN 978 1 78592 758 4
eISBN 978 1 78450 615 5

Printed and bound in Great Britain

To Noah:
From my heart to yours

Noah Langholz 1991–2013

CONTENTS

HEALING MIND-BODY PRACTICES AND CREATIVE ACTIVITIES FOR SURVIVORS

ACKNOWLEDGEMENTS

They will bear you up on their palms, lest you stumble on a stone.

Psalm 91

I'm deeply grateful to all the people who lifted me up and urged me on after Noah's suicide and while writing this book.

First, to my husband, Bryan, who knows the love for Noah and the pain of losing him like no other, my most profound thanks for being by my side in love and darkness and for managing to read the tough parts of this book. I can't imagine this journey without you. And to my beautiful son, Ben, thank you for the hugs and visits and lessons on how people grieve differently. May you cherish your precious life and memories of your little brother.

I'm eternally grateful to my cousin, Renée Schwartz, and dear friends, Jessi Rowe, Claire Gorfinkel, Ellen Dinerman, and Anne Sylvester for being my grief sharers and cheerleaders-in-chief in these difficult years. And to Noah's "other mothers," Rosa Cesaretti and Véronique Waisblat, who loved Noah as their own, thank you for understanding the enormity of this loss.

To my family, especially Sheri Stark, Melanie Langholz, Ike and Faye Langholz, the Langholz-Renshaw family, the Langholz-Hamilton family, Jason Stark, Jon Brock, Wende Brock, Sam and Mala Langholz, Eddy and Laura Langholz, the Fendrich family, Gabe Braun, Peggy Grossman, and Marsha Croland: thank you all for your love and support at key moments in this journey. And to Noah's host family in France, Philippe Carpène, Véronique

Waisblat, Charlie Carpène, and Léo Carpène, *merci et bisous* for sharing this loss with us like family.

To my friends Trudy Baltz, Joyce Burstein, Patty Dobiesz, Jane and Yudie Fishman, Harvey Goldman, Meg Goldman, Larry Goldstein, Jane Hirschkowitz, Kathy Kobayashi, Chris Motley, Susan Neiman, Amy Nettleton, Brina Peck, Sarah Porubcansky, Andra Rose, Joanne Scherr, Ruth Several, Julie Simon, Esther Warkov, Nancy Wiedlin, and Steven Youra, who stepped up in ways both large and small, sustaining me with your friendship and your belief in what I have to say: I so appreciate all that you do. Your engagement with my grief and my blog deepened my understanding and gave me the courage to write this book.

I'm indebted to my fellow survivors of suicide loss in Los Angeles, especially support group co-facilitators Marilyn Nobori and Nina Gutin at Didi Hirsch Mental Health Services, as well as Melody Cotrel, Joerg and Belle Fiederer, Mary Gayman, Rick Moguil, Lisa Richards, Jean Toh, Tina Vartanian, Mary Wallace, Laurie Woodrow, and Rev. Alice Zulli for teaching me how to move through grief and for pointing me toward hope and community. I'm especially grateful to Dr. Nina Gutin for opening doors to survivor authors and experts in the field. And heartfelt thanks to my fellow mourning mom, Barbara Pequet, and her husband, Jim Wallace, who have been so open hearted and understanding as we move through this journey together.

To my therapists, especially Linda Pillsbury and Elisabeth Eilers, and my yoga teacher, Gillian Symonds, thank you for the tools, comfort, and guidance. (And lest I forget Lobo and Miso: thanks for the pup therapy.)

To the entire Pasadena Jewish Temple and Center community, especially Rabbi Joshua Levine-Grater, Rabbi Gil Kollin, Cantor Ruth Berman-Harris, and the Tuesday morning meditators, thank you so much for the hugs, gentle words, moving songs, and dinners left at the door. You gave me reason to keep the faith.

To my fellow survivor bloggers Marjorie Antus, Janie Cook, and Shaye Nelson, thank you for helping me find my voice on the blog. To poet Cathie Sandstrom and authors, Bree Barton, Dave Davis, and Yelizaveta Renfro, as well as the writers in Lisa's class, I greatly appreciate the feedback and the practical tips on publishing. To those who read and helped edit the manuscript, especially Meg Goldman, *mil gracias*. To Iris Bolton, Carla Fine, Dr. William Feigelman, and Dr. John Jordan, I'm indebted to you for reviewing the manuscript and offering your endorsement. And to Elen Griffiths, Emily Badger, and everyone at Jessica Kingsley Publishers, thank you for believing in this book and bringing it to the world.

Finally, a big shout out to Noah's friends—especially Sadie Amelia, Rob Carrington, Vasco Cesaretti, Rachel Connor, Austen Fiora, Sam Fishman, Bennett Kayser, Aaron Khandros, Tom Lee, Kevin O'Neill, Anna Rajo-Miller, Filippo Riviera, John Schmidt, Anne Stellar, Joannice Thevenon, and Avery Trufelman—for loving and missing my son, sharing your memories with Bryan and me, and keeping Noah's spirit alive.

PREFACE

My younger son, Noah Langholz, took his life on March 19, 2013, two days after running the Los Angeles Marathon. He was 21 and had been struggling with major depression and anxiety for about two years, triggered by the suicide of a close friend. When Noah came home from college on medical leave, my husband and I assumed it was to rest and heal. We later realized that he came home to die, and the marathon was his last hurrah. This book bears witness to the first three and a half years after this devastating loss as I poured out my pain and tried to make meaning of what happened.

If you've found your way to this book after losing someone to suicide, my heart is with you. What you're going through is likely the hardest thing you'll ever face. You may be wondering how you can survive the pain, whether it will ever get better (it will, slowly), whether you're crazy (you're not), and what's possible now. I share guideposts from my grief journey in the hope that they can bring recognition, light, and hope to your path, reminding you that you're not alone.

This book is meant for my fellow suicide survivors (those who've lost close family and friends to suicide), as well as those who love and care for them. It's also for anyone who wishes to better understand survivors or the trajectories of young people who are struggling, including professionals in the health, mental health, education, religion, and law enforcement arenas. While part of the book deals directly with losing a child, most of it is relevant to any type of suicide loss and much of it pertains to grief generally, especially complicated grief after a sudden death.

This book grew out of a blog I began three months after Noah's death, *Walking the Mourner's Path After a Child's Suicide*, with the idea of the mourner's path inspired by the work of Anne Brener (2012). I felt compelled to publicly express my grief and explore universal aspects of suicide loss in the hope of helping others and myself. The blog has connected me with fellow survivors who share their stories; it has also deepened my bond with friends and family who follow my story with encouragement. Writing the blog and this book has been essential to the healing I've managed to find thus far. Psychologists might call my writings "ruminations" that are part of the process of "post-traumatic growth," discussed in the final chapter.

Unlike many survivors, I've lived this nightmare before. My father died by suicide when he was 55 and I was 26. He was proof that clinical depression could be a terminal disease, but somehow I forgot that lesson years later as I helplessly watched my child's decline. I was proof that family members could survive and heal after suicide loss, and that lesson informed much of how I responded to Noah's suicide. On the other hand, squeezed between losing a father and a child to suicide, I felt doubly cursed by abandonment and betrayal. I write about the counterpoint between these two enormous losses in Chapter 1 and throughout the book.

Unlike survivors' accounts that are written in retrospect many years after the tragedy, most of this book was written in real time during the first few years after the suicide that survivors tend to find most difficult. To authentically chronicle my experience, I've retained the essence of early reflections that I may see differently now, sometimes adding additional commentary or information in parenthetical notes. I hope the immediacy and honesty of my reflections on the early, most intense stages of suicide loss will resonate with readers at any stage in the process. For longer-term perspectives, please see the later entries within each chapter, the quotes from experts and seasoned survivors, and the References and Recommended Resources sections.

Also unlike many grief memoirs, this book is organized thematically rather than chronologically. I hope this will make it easy for you to turn to the topics you need at the moment since everyone's grief timetable is unique. Within each thematic chapter, the reflections are in chronological order (@ 6 months, @ 24 months) to show how that aspect of the experience unfolded over time. The chapters are arranged roughly in the order that I became most concerned with each topic, from shock at the beginning to reintegration and the "new normal" toward the end. Suicide grief is not a linear process but an iterative one that goes back and forth, with no finish line. I continued wrestling with most of the issues in this book over the three and a half years.

Please read this book in whatever way is helpful to you. My guess is you'll want to read relevant chapters separately, tracing the journey on that particular theme, then taking a break; this is especially important if you're recently bereaved and need to "dose" your grief in manageable amounts. The first chapter introduces three touchstones that resonate throughout the book: the circumstances of Noah's suicide; my father's suicide 31 years earlier; and my efforts to reach out to fellow survivors. If you've recently lost a loved one, you might begin with "Letter to the Newly Bereaved" at the end of Chapter 1 and Chapter 2: The Body Takes a Hit. If you're worried about how to handle a birthday or holiday, see Chapter 5: Forever 21 and Chapter 7: Grief Holiday. If you're tormented with self-blame, Chapter 6: Living the Nightmare and Chapter 11: The Hard Stuff may help. If you're a friend or professional trying to help someone after suicide loss, you might have a look at Chapter 3: What They Say and Don't Say, Chapter 10: Soothing Our Grieving Selves, and Chapter 14: "Climbing into the Day" to get oriented.

Whatever your circumstances, if you're a survivor, I hope you'll try some of the healing mind-body exercises and creative activities featured at the end of each chapter. Most are adapted from yoga, meditation, mindfulness, Qi Gong, and other therapeutic practices that I've found helpful. They can be tools for coping with grief that lodges in the body, beyond the reach of words. I also urge you to use a journal for your own reflections.

This book documents my personal experience and doesn't claim to be authoritative about suicide, suicide loss, mental health conditions, grief, or healing. I've learned a lot about these things since Noah's death, including getting trained in suicide awareness, suicide grief, and bereavement group facilitation, but there's still much to learn. I include information from experts and other survivors that I hope will inform and inspire you. I also include poetry that may speak to you more directly than prose. All poems in this book are my own unless attributed to others.

Many people today look to grief memoirs as "our primers in the logic and ethics of mourning," writes memoirist Meghan O'Rourke (2015, p. 16). "These books teach us that grief is not something merely to endure, medicate away or 'muscle through,' but an essential aspect of life—even a kind of privilege."

It's a privilege to share my grief journey with you. Thank you for turning to this book. To my fellow survivors: may it help in your own quest for comfort, courage, and clarity. Let's continue the conversation to see where our paths may cross. I invite you to share your story and your response to this book by commenting on my blog or my website.[1]

Finally, let's use our understanding of suicide to raise awareness to prevent more tragic loss of life and the devastation of suicide for other families and communities. All royalties from this book will go to the Noah Langholz Remembrance Fund to support suicide prevention and postvention programs and research.

---

1   http://afterachildssuicide.blogspot.com and www.susanauerbachwriter.com

PROLOGUE: HAPPIER DAYS

Noah: The story of this book begins with your ending. But we must remember this: the happier days of your beginning and middle.

Just two months after you were born in 1991 in Pasadena, California, we got your first passport and left for Dad's sabbatical year in Cambridge, England. You were a Gerber baby with blond wisps framing your round face; we called you Pudge. I stuffed you into snowsuits and took you to the park in all kinds of weather, packed with your big brother, Ben, into a double buggy with rain covers. Your first beach was in Wales, your first wobbly steps on the plane coming back to the US. As a child, you sent little boats made of twigs down the stream in Norway and swam with sea turtles in the Galapagos. You were always a traveler.

You gravitated to animals, from snails and lizards to our long-lived family dog, Wags. You dressed Wags up in hats and sunglasses; draped yourself over her when she lay down; drew her endlessly for school art projects. You befriended every pet you met, even the mean ones.

You grew up in the snug surround of family. Ben made everything exciting, whether shooting water balloons and making odd constructions out of scrap wood in the backyard or playing Legos and later, video games when Dad and I finally said yes. You and Dad made the world's best latkes at Nana and Papa's huge Chanukah parties, where there were always lots of cousins. *It may sound strange to have my grandpa in the same list as Gandhi,* you wrote in a high school essay, *but he is a highly influential figure in my life. Even after being through many hardships, he uses his wisdom and uncontrollable tendency to make friends with everyone he meets to live his life to the fullest.* So did you.

So many passions you pursued! You and Ben learned model rocketry and juggling from Dad, along with the fearlessness to try new things. At nine, you practiced juggling three balls 100 times till you had no drops; soon, you made five-ball tricks or flaming torches look easy. *During my free time I like to watch films, cook, go hiking, read, take photographs, ride bicycle and whenever possible go to the beach,* you wrote at 17. *I also love playing water sports, and I go surfing whenever I can.* With water polo and surfing, you morphed from a gawky, narrow-shouldered kid to a smooth-muscled teen—what a friend of mine called a "dreamboat" with dark, curly hair, green eyes, and thick, arched eyebrows over a Roman nose.

You were a connoisseur of conversation and of friends, always ready to engage or to go out and have fun. In our years-long conversation, you and I covered film, art, politics, friends, sex, religion. You could argue a position even if you knew little about the topic, like a lawyer without a brief. You could talk all night with old friends or new friends and chat with anyone—aging Vietnam vets at a Veterans Administration hospital, tough motorcycle club riders at a roadside tavern.

School came easy for you as a child, though what really got your attention was running with a pack of boys on the playground. As a teen, you learned best from friends, foreign films, other cultures. You reinvented yourself during study abroad in your senior year of high school while living with a French family on a houseboat near Paris. You ate Nutella on baguette for breakfast, leaped over Metro turnstiles, learned French accordion, and even started to look French. You transformed yourself again at Wesleyan University in Connecticut, where you found wonderful friends, joined the sailing team, studied Arabic and architecture, worked as a film projectionist, and became a photography major. With your lanky 6'4" frame, you were conspicuous on the small campus; they called you Daddy Longlegs.

You had your first bout with depression, as far as Dad and I knew, in France after a breakup. Your serious struggles began after a close friend at college died by suicide and you took a year off from school to live in San Francisco.

At that time, you and your brother, Ben, were just starting to bond again after living separate teenage lives. Ben helped you get settled in the city, where he was finishing school and soon to start work as a designer at Facebook. You got an internship at an architecture firm, then drifted for a while before going back to school the next fall. Meanwhile, Dad and I were filling our empty nest in Altadena, California, with a new dog, four chickens, and Dad's gardening projects, while both working as professors. I was active in our synagogue and learning to write poetry.

"Whatever you do, Mom," you said one day in late 2012, "don't publish any poems about me." This seemed odd since I'd never shown you my work or published any poems. Now I wonder: Were you already talking with the end in mind?

You knew me too well. Of course, I would have to write about you. There's so much to apologize for, but not this. After suicide, the needs of the living come first.

Moving Ground

It was the time when the salamanders
appeared underfoot, fresh from their primeval
lair, their nude red-brown forms lumbering
into the brush with a backward glance.

My young son saw the ground move,
dove to catch one—a prize in his palm.
He stared and stroked the gelatinous shape,
awaiting a message from dinosaur time
while hiking his first whine-less mile.

I miss that boy who stooped to inspect
every worm and lizard in his path.
Does he still pick them up, amazed
at his luck, barely daring to breathe?

He stumbles into the thicket of his twenties
without a backward glance.

Noah, about age 4, with the author.

Noah, 11, juggling clubs with his dad, Bryan, and Aunt Lynn.

Noah, 14, with his beloved Wags.

Noah, 17, right, backpacking in Sequoia National Forest with his dad, Bryan, center, and friend, Sammy, left.

Noah, 18, right, with grandparents, Ike and Faye, center, brother, Ben, back left, and cousins, Bridget, Jason, and Sasha, at one of many extended family gatherings.

Last photo of our family of four, 2010, with Ben on left, Noah on right.

Untitled black and white photo by Noah Langholz, 2012.

Chapter 1

STEPPING INTO THE WILDERNESS

Is sorrow all I have left of you
Besides the wall your name is carved into
I'm not trying to get over
I'm just trying to get through
All I've got is a hole
In the shape of you

essence and Jeffrey Pease, "Shape of You" (2009)

The First Horrific Days

Note: This first section contains disturbing images.

On the Tuesday when everything changed, I dawdle at work later than usual. I dread facing our troubled son and the pall of depression that engulfs our home.

Three weeks earlier, Noah had come home from college on medical leave, looking gaunt as a refugee. He'd been unable to function at the school he loved after a psychotic episode and a mounting sense of shame over aggressively pursuing a young woman who rejected him ("everyone knows there's something wrong with me"). For three weeks at home, he's been mostly watching TV, his world of adventure shrunk to the den and an occasional chess game with his dad. Noah has said little and contacted no one, barely smiled or laughed. It's been months since he saw a therapist or tried meds for depression;

he hasn't told us about his terrifying anxiety attacks. My husband, Bryan, and I give him a wide berth, afraid to push. We assume he'll be himself again with time and help, but I'm getting impatient. After all, he managed to run a marathon two days before, carrying on a family tradition. I've been reminding him to call a psychiatrist and get a part-time job. I don't see that he can't even pick up the phone to make an appointment.

As I open the front door that Tuesday and call out to Noah, there's no answer, no TV blare. The house is empty. No response to my phone call or text either. A flutter of worry rises in my gut. Maybe he's taken his motorcycle or bike for a ride? I head outside to the garage to check.

As I lift the garage door, I see two bare feet dangling over the table where no human feet should be, attached to a shape hanging from the rafters. I'm so shocked that at first, I don't recognize Noah's body; I think someone has put up an effigy of him as a prank, draped in his jeans and a flowing white shirt I've never seen before. His dark, curly head is bent to the side, full lips parted. His bloodshot eyes bulge with astonishment, as if to say: *This is what it's like?*

NO, NO—not our beautiful boy.

I scream and run in circles, blood surging, brain frozen. *Phone, phone, where is my phone?* I run inside to call Bryan and 911 but I drop my cell phone and it goes blank.

Now I'm crying and screaming and our neighbor, John, comes running, huffing heavily. "Oh, God, oh, God," he moans when he sees Noah. He heaves himself up on the table and calls for a knife to cut Noah down as he pulls on the knot.

What is a knife? Where is a knife? I fumble around in the hardware cabinet till I find big scissors. John saws at the rope, still moaning.

"I'm gonna need you to catch him," he says, and I move in as close as I can to Noah's feet. John eases Noah's body down into my arms. He's still warm, taut with muscle and bone, the heaviest thing I've ever held. I clutch him to me upright and still. The baby I delivered into the world, squirming, now a young man delivered into my embrace, inert.

We lay Noah on his back on the cold, cement floor of the garage. His long limbs sprawl over half its length. John kneels over him and talks himself through the steps of CPR. "OK, OK, clear windpipe first." His wife stands outside in the driveway, calling 911 and crying.

I sit on the floor by Noah's head, useless. I wish I could hold him in my lap but I'll just get in John's way. *Please let him live, please.* All I hear is John's labored puffs—no rousing gurgle of life. I can't bear to look at Noah's open eyes or the burn mark on his neck. "It's OK, Noah," I say, over and over, stroking his hair, but I know that nothing's OK. Paramedics arrive with equipment on wheels, then police and a crowd in the street.

Bryan's car pulls up and I bolt down the driveway to reach him first. He's getting a bag of rotisserie chicken out of the back seat. I grab his arm and blurt out the hardest words I've ever had to say: "Noah hung himself in the garage!"

Bryan's face contorts. "Oh, no!" He drops the bag and dashes for the garage, where he crouches beside Noah.

More sirens, and the police turn the driveway into a crime scene. They won't let us stay in the garage. We watch its shadowy interior from a distance, barely breathing ourselves. Finally, the paramedics emerge to say that Noah's gone. Bryan and I rock and sob, each alone in our nightmare.

Bryan's sisters arrive with stricken faces and start the hard work of making "sad news" calls to family and strangers. It must be 6pm, maybe 7. Shaking, I call good friends who live nearby; as soon as I croak, "Noah killed himself," they say they'll be right over. They and others show up at the door, shifting from foot to foot in silence. I cry, hug, send e-mails, retreat. *How can this be?*

We wait hours for the coroner, the police and caution tape still outside. Bryan scans Noah's phone and laptop before handing them over to the police as "evidence." There's no note, no trail of despair.

Our older son, Ben, arrives by plane at midnight. My in-laws are driving home as fast as they can from a trip to, of all places, Death Valley, California. We're stumbling through the valley of death that we never imagined was so close.

The next few days are a blur of pain, disbelief, and logistics. I feel socked in the gut, slapped in the face. I keep replaying the scene in the garage in my mind, especially when alone or lying down, and have to yell, "Stop it!" Every morning I come awake for a few seconds before I remember with a thud that Noah's dead. I gaze out at the empty driveway and picture him appearing at the gate and walking toward me, saying it was all a bad dream. I'm not yet asking *why* so much as *what happened* and *how could you?* How I wish he'd kept his feet on the ground.

Instinctively, as if programmed by my father's suicide 31 years earlier, I attend to arrangements and other people's grief. I'm mortified that Noah betrayed so many people who loved him and feel I owe them some apology or explanation. Noah's adored 80-year-old grandfather, for one, a Holocaust survivor who spent decades rebuilding family and hope after devastation, only to outlive his grandson. "Things will never be the same," he mutters, shaking his head. I pass around a reading from the psychiatrist Kay Jamison on how people intent on suicide are, at some point, beyond the reach of love or therapy. I want to believe it so Noah's act won't hurt so much. But I'm his mother. *I should have seen the signs and known how to help him.*

I want to flee from every step of the funeral. Choosing Noah's favorite T-shirt for burial, the shrunken bright yellow one with "Ike & Sam's" on a California license plate, a reminder of the liquor store his grandfather and great-uncle used to own. Using Noah's college fund to buy a last-minute cemetery plot, with plots of our own a few feet away so we can be near Noah in death, if not in life. Hearing Ben wail when the casket is opened; seeing Noah-but-not-Noah one last time, his jaw grimly set, his tall frame crammed into the box. Dimly registering the speeches at the service but having no words of my own. Refusing to look as the box carrying our child is lowered into the earth; hurrying away before shovelfuls of dirt are heaped on top of it and people approach us, speechless about an unspeakable act.

In the next few weeks, Bryan and I, fortunate to be excused from work, are overwhelmed with condolence cards, "checking in" e-mails, and chicken or salmon dinners left on the doorstep.

(A considerate cousin brings a meal labeled, "NOT chicken or salmon.") I can't read or watch anything but escapist TV. I can't meditate or even breathe deep for more than a minute without crying. I avoid looking at the garage and wish we could tear it down; we put up a makeshift bamboo screen to block it from view. I can't handle the speed of driving, the bright lights of the supermarket. I squeeze my eyes shut while others drive for fear I'll glimpse a young man on the street that looks like Noah. Even the "sustainable" label on one of his college notebooks made from recycled paper triggers anguish. Why couldn't Noah have been made of sustainable material?

I'm cast into the wilderness with no idea which way to go or how to bear it. I know only that I must keep moving through it—and chart my course in words. I take Noah's unfinished notebook and title it 'Mourning Book #1'. I'll fill eight of these before I'm ready to call them 'Mourning and Living Books'.

I started a blog three months after Noah's death, but I never wrote about the day of his suicide there. By that time, I was working hard in therapy to purge myself of traumatic thoughts. I shrank from other survivors' descriptions of the method and scene of suicides; I couldn't stand the reminders or watch other families suffer.

As I recall those desperate days now, I realize two things: I wish someone had given me a map of the wilderness I was entering. And I already had a map, faded and sketchy, from my father's suicide that I hadn't looked at in years and couldn't bear to unfold after Noah's suicide. There was simply no room in my shattered heart to hold both losses.

The next section describes my father's suicide and how it both eased and complicated my grief journey with Noah. This is followed by a letter to the newly bereaved that I wish I could have received.

Déjà-vu: How Can This Be Happening...Again?

I've been here before. I flashed on this thought several times in the hours after Noah's suicide. *This is how it is*—the shock, the endless tears and whys and what-ifs. *This is what you do*—make calls, search for a note, plan a service. I watched my husband crumple, thrust into an unknown hell, while I moved numbly past familiar landmarks. *How can this be happening...again?*

My father, Irwin Auerbach, took his life on May 30, 1982, when he was 55 and I was 26. I don't know how long he lived with depression, only that on Wednesday nights in my childhood when I was told he was at a union meeting, he was actually seeing a psychiatrist. As a teenager, I noticed his smile looked half-hearted or overblown. I found out later from his writings that he made himself do "laugh therapy" late at night with *New Yorker* cartoons and TV talk shows. He thought he'd be happier after divorcing my mother and retiring early from his bureaucrat's job at the Social Security Administration, but he always seemed like a lonely soul.

When I was 14, I came home from school to find half the books and records gone and a note on the kitchen table. *I need some time alone*, it said, *you can call me at work. Irv/Dad.* No *Love.* I stayed angry for years at my father for leaving my mother and me. I hated having to spend time alone with him at Friday dinners out and summer excursions, right at the age when I wanted to be on my own or with friends. I resented having to justify expenses like college tuition to his penny-pinching judgment. We began to call a truce after my mother died five years later, but still fell easily into bickering.

My father and I got along best through letters. He'd honed a clear, succinct style while aspiring to journalism as a young man, and he always encouraged my writing. When I was in college, he'd send my letters back with edits, which I took as a sign of love. Later, he was my most faithful correspondent when I was living in a Greek mountain village doing folk music research. In terse paragraphs with ALL CAPS, he wrote of jazz concerts he attended, treatments he tried for back pain, all the reasons for him not to retrain as a librarian. I tried to cheer him with my blue aerograms, regaling him with village gossip and urging him to follow his dream of opening a bookstore. I hinted I was ready to forgive him, but maybe my signal was weak.

I didn't know how much my father was suffering till a telegram arrived in the village: *Being treated for severe depression. Call home.* When I did, he sounded desperate and disoriented, and I arranged to fly home. The night before my arrival, my father drove to a nearby lake, left his wallet in the car, and drowned himself. My uncle identified my father for police; I never saw the body.

There's no good way to find out about a suicide.

My uncle picked me up two hours late from National Airport with a garbled apology. We were halfway back to my father's apartment in Columbia, Maryland, when my uncle said he had bad news. "Your father went out to Wilde Lake last night and didn't come back." My uncle's eyes stayed steady on the highway. "A jogger found his body at 6am this morning."

I stared down at the floor of the car, unable to speak, fighting to breathe. My father, dead? How could he do this when I was on my way home to help him? I was an only child, a motherless child; how could my father destroy my last vestige of family?

At my father's funeral, as at Noah's, there was crying and stunned silence, with me too broken to make a speech. I learned a lot about my father that day. I knew he'd been a civil rights activist and outspoken advocate of civil liberties, but I didn't know so many people admired him. "He was the brave one," his old friend and fellow activist began, standing up at the service before breaking down. "I just don't understand." It was much like Noah's friends who called my son a "Bunsen burner of joy" with "a big laugh, a big heart, big ideas, and a curious spirit." They couldn't square Noah's charisma and love of life with ending it.

Flying west across the Atlantic to see my father in 1982, I'd been tense with dread, unsure of what sort of father I'd find at home and how I'd be expected or able to help him. I'd never heard him so scared and confused as on that phone call. I hadn't known his diagnosis of severe depression until that week and had never seen him, or anyone, in that state.

Flying across the US on a red-eye to fetch Noah home from college in 2013, my heart began thumping wildly as we neared the east coast. Noah had sounded so dejected and disjointed when he called to say he needed to come home. What sort of Noah would I find in his dorm? Would he even be there? A terrible sense of déjà-vu loomed like a tidal wave: Would the same fate await me as on that other plane ride? Before the wave could swamp me, I turned away and wrenched open the window shade. Pale streaks of sunrise, ever more luminous, were bearing the plane towards morning. As I watched, the wave subsided. I prayed that Noah would find a window on beauty in the world again.

After their suicides, I became the curator of my father's and son's lives. I told what little I knew to rabbis for the eulogy. I fielded condolence calls and messages under a cloud of unspoken questions. I pored through both men's papers and belongings and talked with their therapists, searching for clues. I learned that the week before my father's suicide, he'd been agitated about his psychologist's plan to hospitalize him as soon as a bed became available. Though it would have been an unlocked ward in a general hospital, my father had always been suspicious of doctors and institutions, much like Noah. The new anti-depressants in my father's system that were starting to ease his mood may have given him the energy to take action, as with many suicides.

I assembled a packet of bits of my father's youthful poetry and mid-life jottings and sent them to his friends: *Alone with pain again/Calm piano comes through./Warm coffee comes through./Alone with pain again.* I wanted there to be more of my father to give to the world, and this was all that was left.

I assumed I'd do the same with Noah's writings, but they were sparse and confusing. Instead, I sent Noah's negatives, contact sheets, and black and white prints to his college friends so they could prepare an exhibit of his photographs. I thumbed through his best 8x10's: a young woman in an abandoned office trailer, her face framed by a hanging grid, set off by side windows that project squares of light on the wall and reveal scenes beyond the frame; an illuminated statue of a Madonna and child in a vestibule behind railings and grillwork, topped with sunspots; a portrait of a beaming, middle-aged Italian hairdresser ringed by several poufy-haired assistants. I couldn't believe that my son's creative life had been reduced to this shallow box, his early attempts now his final work. I compiled lines from his friends' memories and sent them to our friends and family: *For Noah, every moment was an experience worth having and every person was worth sharing it with.*

After Noah's death, I was haunted by the symmetry of being doubly cursed by suicide. I was in my twenties when I lost my father; Noah was in his twenties when he took his life. My father was in his fifties when he died by suicide; I was in my fifties when I lost Noah. Both the man who raised me and the child who I raised abandoned me. Both as an adult child with my parents and as a parent with my younger son, I would never share an adult relationship, celebrate milestones, enjoy grandchildren, give or take comfort in old age.

I've been here before. Two highly intelligent, articulate men with clinical depression who mostly resisted treatment and hid their suicidal thoughts. The lost chance for reconciliation. The same two old friends who flew to my side like sisters when they heard the news.

But the old map from my father's suicide only took me so far with Noah; it didn't go deep into trauma territory. I never saw my father's decline, and I never saw him dead. I witnessed all that with Noah plus my own helplessness and guilt in the face of his struggle. I was both more thoroughly shaken by Noah's suicide and more equipped to deal with it.

Returning to the US without home or family in 1982, I knew I had to get on with my life in spite of—and because of—my father's suicide. I had to prove to myself that I wasn't like him and wouldn't end up like him. I moved back to Seattle, where I had a Master's degree to finish. While out dancing, I promptly broke my ankle and was housebound for months. I holed up in my apartment and eked out pages of my thesis on Greek women's songs and laments. As I translated the traditional laments I had collected, I cried them for my father: *With one tear, say it; with one word, expel it/ Whoever has lost her parents loses her returning home.* The only suicide survivor at a grief retreat, I couldn't talk about a loss that seemed to spook others. I was groping in the dark, waiting for time to do its work.

When Noah took his life, I sensed that if I had to live this nightmare again, I'd experience it fully awake, knowing that I would survive. This time, I had a family of my own, a community where I'd lived for 25 years, a career as a professor. This time, my grief was shared, though my husband and I also cried apart, wary of upsetting the other, and my son, Ben, was mostly stoic during his visits. I could call on survivor support groups, the Internet, and a growing literature on suicide loss, none of which were available in 1982. Hearing stories of fellow survivors greatly lessened the fear, stigma, and isolation the second time around. At 57, I found comfort in yoga, meditation, Shabbat, and Jewish mourning rituals that I didn't appreciate at 26. And I revived my long-dormant writer's voice by starting a blog.

For a long time after Noah killed himself, I avoided thinking about my father's suicide. I went to survivors' gatherings so focused on losing a child that it took hearing others talk about losing parents to jolt me into remembering that I'm also a survivor of my father's suicide. An early draft of this book only mentioned my father in passing. The longer I live with the loss of my child, the more I find I can open my heart to reclaim the loss of my father. To set my father's picture on the table next to Noah's and weep for both of them. To own that I'm twice a survivor of suicide and that these formative experiences bracket my adult life.

No map is ever enough when thrust into the wilderness of suicide loss. At least the old map I had from after my father's death reminded me that I could survive. Those of us who've lost loved ones to suicide need to pass on whatever maps we have. Here's one I sketched for the friend of a friend, who lost her 27-year-old son to suicide two years after we lost Noah. If you, too, are a survivor of suicide, I hope the letter and the rest of this book guide you to the mileposts I wish I'd known about when my father and my son took their lives.

Letter to the Newly Bereaved

Dear Friend:

I'm so very sorry for your loss. I don't know anything about you, your loved one, or your situation. I don't know how you've grieved in the past or how you'll grieve now. But I know that if you're bereaved by suicide, you're likely in shock, traumatized, and hurt beyond measure. I hope you find something here that resonates with you and reminds you that you're not alone in this terrible place.

How can this be happening? Whatever your loved one's history and state of mind, however much you knew or did not know about it, you're in a state of shock and disbelief. You may feel numb or fall apart. You may feel physically assaulted, as if crushed by a huge stone or suddenly missing a limb. You may not be able to focus or reason, to eat or sleep or breathe properly. You think the world will never be the same, and you're right—but in ways you can't yet imagine. In the wake of this tragedy, you may find more love, generosity, and even gratitude than you thought possible.

I just want to crawl in a hole. Be gentle with yourself and with the mourners close to you. Give yourself permission to hibernate for a while if you wish. With your own urgent need for comfort, it can be tough to comfort family members; try to leave that to others. If you have a spouse or partner, each of you may need to grope your own way through grief. Give each other space and be there for each other when you're able, with faith that you'll be more present for one another in time.

I don't even know what I need right now. Let people know what happened so they can take care of you. Ask for help and accept the support that's offered on your terms; it's OK to say "no thanks" or "not now." You're released from all social obligations and hopefully, from work or other obligations during the first weeks after the suicide.

I have no energy. The body takes a hit. Don't be surprised if your health goes haywire. This is where shock takes root. Go slow. Walk around the block. Allow yourself naps or quiet resting time. Remember to breathe. Meditate even for a few minutes with a guided meditation for healing. Find a doctor who understands that you're suffering from shock and grief and can help explain this to your boss if you need time off.

I can't stop crying. Don't fear tears. Let them flow through you, washing you clean like a rain till the next storm. It helps to know there's someone you can call, a piece of music you can play, or a faith community you can visit to steady yourself. Find an expressive release; write, draw, dance, run, pray out your grief. Shout and pound out your anger, too; it's natural to feel abandoned and betrayed. Let it out.

Why? How? What if? Questions rush in. You're searching for clues, even if you know you'll never know anything certain. We need to search as long as we feel the need. Our task as mourners is to build a "coherent narrative" of the suicide that is "compassionate and bearable," according to psychologist John Jordan (2011, pp. 182, 199). This takes time.

I should have, could have, would have… Self-blame may haunt you. Especially if you lost a child, you may feel that you failed in your most fundamental duty as a parent. None of us are mind readers; all of us are flawed; mental illness, when present, can be formidable. Breathe in compassion for yourself and for your lost one. We can't forgive ourselves until we forgive them, and vice versa. That can be the longest, hardest road. If you have a spiritual practice, try to reclaim it bit by bit, even if you're angry at God or the universe.

What now? Therapy can help, preferably with a professional trained in grief and suicide loss. Consider mind-body treatments like EMDR (Eye Movement Desensitization and Reprocessing) to deal with your intense feelings and guide you through post-traumatic shock into "post-traumatic growth." Do yoga or tai chi to keep the energy moving.

Where's hope? Probably still a ways off. Take heart from grief expert Alan Wolfelt (2009), who says that you can be the source of your own hope: "You create hope in yourself by actively mourning the death and setting your intention to heal" (p. 10). And from the author Helen Macdonald (2014), who discovered many months after her father's death: "There was no patience in my waiting, but time had passed all the same, and worked its careful magic. And now…all the grief had turned into something different. It was simply love" (p. 268).

Truly, you are not alone. There's a community of suicide loss survivors that will reach out to you and share their journey toward healing. Take what hope and healing you can from books and online resources on suicide loss. When you're ready, check out local support groups for survivors or online forums like Alliance of Hope (see the Recommended Resources at the end of the book). Whenever we survivors share our stories, it's indeed an alliance of hope that we create together.

Right now, you're as hurt and broken as a person can be. Know that you won't always feel this way. Keep moving through your grief. Reach out for love and support; there's a lot of it out there.

Wishing you comfort and courage,
Susan

TO MY FELLOW SURVIVORS:
If you've lost someone recently to suicide, I hope it helps to have a map. See also the tips in Iris Bolton's well-known list, "Beyond Surviving: Suggestions for Survivors" (on page 202 at the end of this book). Remember to pace yourself and "dose" your grief in small batches as you read the chapters that speak to your needs.

Calming the Breath

Suicide loss survivors often suffer from racing hearts and constricted breathing, so many of the exercises offered in this book focus on breath. These two simple yoga techniques (adapted from yoga practices) can help calm the breath after a grief wave, before a stressful activity, or at bedtime. Begin by sitting quietly with eyes closed; try to repeat each pattern for at least a few minutes to feel the benefits.

Belly Breathing

- Slowly inhale and feel the belly expand as it fills with air for three beats.

- Hold the breath for three beats.

- As you exhale slowly, feel the belly contract toward your spine for three beats.

- Suspend the breath out for three beats and repeat the pattern.

Alternate Nostril Breathing

- With your right thumb over your *right* nostril (closing it), inhale slowly through your left nostril for three beats.

- Now lift off the thumb and close your *left* nostril with your right index finger as you exhale through the right nostril for three beats.

- Reverse: Keeping your right index finger where it is (over the left nostril), inhale through your right nostril for three beats.

- Finally, with your right thumb again over your *right* nostril, exhale through your left nostril for three beats and repeat the four-part pattern.

Chapter 2

THE BODY TAKES A HIT
Shock and Tears

Your loss undermines the rhythm and disrupts the momentum of the flow of your life… One day you will breathe fully into life again, but just now you cannot imagine it… One day you will choose to live again fully by finding the courage to be whole despite your sorrow.

Rev. Alice Zulli (2014)

The Body Takes a Hit—@ 2 months

Life has been suspended for weeks, frozen in shock on March 19 and the anguished days that have followed. It feels like my skin is ripped off, my heart blasted out, my leg amputated. While still overcome with shock, I can barely grasp my grief.

All bodily systems are stop—respiratory, cardiovascular, immune, digestive. My chest feels weighted by a constant stone, wheezing my breath out through a straw. A bad cold won't heal, sapping my energy even for a walk around the block or a short visit with friends. A simple bang to the foot turns into piercing pain at night. I need long naps every day. I literally can't stomach Noah's suicide.

I've never been to the doctor so often or cried in the doctor's office. To my amazement, the doctor took my hands in hers and listened to my story with her full attention, telling me nothing was in my imagination and I should come in as often as necessary to talk. In her notes, she listed the reason for the visit as "grief reaction." "Have people been telling you there's a silver lining?" she asked. "Because there's not. This is ugly and horrible and the worst thing that will ever happen to you." I nodded, startled by her frankness. She asked what I was doing to take care of myself and told me about the book, *When the Body Says No*. I walked out of her office feeling strangely calm. (And found out later that this doctor lost her mother to suicide when she was 12.)

The body will no doubt say no again. Meanwhile, I'm seizing the bit of energy that has returned.

Emerging—@ 3 months

Life is starting to move on in fits and starts without Noah in it.

This week, I went to the movies for the first time. I started to wear colors again rather than drab and to think about getting a haircut. I can finally read parts of the newspaper without feeling totally assaulted by violence and death. I can pass young people on the street without always thinking ruefully of Noah. Sometimes, I can even hear friends recount news of their kids without tuning it all out in a haze of hurt. My attention has just begun to shift from full-time grieving to wondering how to continue grieving while slowly rejoining the flow of life.

I've heard that the period between three months and a year after a suicide can be the hardest time for survivors. The worst of the shock has been absorbed, exposing the raw pain beneath. How to resume normal activities with our souls so broken? How to reconcile the need to grieve with the need to live and the guilt that comes from small moments of distraction? I imagine I'll be writing from both needs in the time to come—and all the places in between.

(Later, I'll learn that mourners vacillate between moving toward grief with a loss orientation and moving away from grief with a restoration orientation, with some people leaning more one way than the other [Jordan and Baugher 2016]. Over time, it's gotten easier for me to pivot between the two—but sometimes it still feels creaking and arduous, like turning a big ship in a tight harbor.)

Welcoming Tears—@ 4 months

The tears of suicide loss aren't like other tears. They're endless and pure and come gushing out many times a day, washing us clean for a moment. They come in silent, heaving bursts that make the face contort and squeeze the breath into short, agitated spurts. When we let out their sound, it's like the howl of a wounded animal. I'd hear those sobs around the house the first few weeks and go running to find my husband, Bryan. I'd close the windows so my own primitive cries wouldn't alarm the neighbors.

This inexhaustible well of tears seems ready to pour out at the slightest reminder. Each outpouring releases a little more of the vastness of grief. I cling to my tears, to what's left of my bond with Noah in the salt tracks on my face.

The hardest days are when work or other obligations compel me to keep tears at bay. Holding back feels unnatural, like damming an untamed river. The tears will have out, if not at the end of the day, then when driving or resting or when a movie or TV drama comes to a poignant end. *Not another ending please.*

In my alternate vision of the day of his death, Noah collapses in tears, unable to follow through on his violent plan. But that would mean he could still feel his bond with the living and give voice to the tender, vulnerable side of himself. We hadn't heard that voice for months. I weep for the loss of that tender soul that could have, maybe, saved his life.

Lessons from Tears—@ 5 months

I'm becoming an expert on tears. What I've learned:

1. There are as many kinds of tears in grief as kinds of snow in the Arctic.

2. You can cry without tears and without sound, just a grimace and an internal shudder.

3. When you lie on your back, tears leak down your temples and into your ears.

4. You can look stricken after a cry, but if you wear glasses, no one will notice.

5. You can get an infection of the eyelids from too much crying. Always carry lubricating eye drops.

6. The purge of a big cry can bring on a purge from your bladder!

7. Best places to cry: in the car, going slow or parked; in bed; in the shower; beside moving water; at a place of prayer; in therapy sessions or survivor support groups.

8. After a really big cry, you feel like you'll dissolve again at any moment for at least a day or two.

9. You can move in and out of crying and still smile at pets and babies and kind people.

10. Tears are a renewable resource. They open the heart and seal the bond with the person you lost.

The Urge to Dance—@ 13 months

A confession: In the weeks before Noah's first death anniversary, I started to feel the urge to dance. It came over me whenever I heard the catchy R&B theme music of a TV show. I'd start wiggling in my seat, then stop, self-conscious. How could I want to dance when I'd been crying a few hours earlier? When I finally stood up to dance through the whole song, I felt liberated, like a submerged creature thrashing up out of the depths.

"There are no rules," a friend told me. "You've got to ride your grief like a wave and see where it takes you."

I browsed through old CDs and searched for tunes that I used to like to dance to with the volume cranked up. I did a lot of folk dancing to Balkan music when I was young, so I was pleased to find a rousing Albanian folk song. Alone in the kitchen, I spun a scarf in the air as if leading the dance line and whirled around with whistles that brought the dog trotting in. I danced furiously, replaying the song over and over, as if emerging from a long confinement. I avoided dancing through the door into the dining room, where we have a little shrine for Noah; I didn't want him watching me.

A time to dance, a time to mourn—I used to think the two were opposites. I often said I learned how to dance and mourn while living in a Greek village researching folk traditions. But what I really learned was the way pathos intertwines with *kefi* (zest for life) and the need to "break out" in self-expression—like the old man in the village square who jumped up to lead the dance about lost youth, his dour face suddenly radiant.

Now when I feel the urge to dance, I try to honor it. It's not so much about being happy and light-hearted as it is about needing to feel alive and let the body speak. The life force that's lain dormant bubbles up like a sustaining spring, in spite of or because of tragic loss. Its arrival gives me hope for the years ahead.

I understand if some are appalled at the thought of dancing while mourning. But if you, too, have felt the urge, you're not alone. Molly Fumia (2012), whose book title, *Safe Passage*, conveys her hope for fellow travelers in grief, wrote (p. 45):

> I lie in the dark, aware that in the distance, the music of life is playing. Even in my grieving for you, I am drawn to the sounds and my body begins to stir.

> Your voice, next to me in the night, gives me a little nudge. "Go ahead. Dance."

> So I stand up, still clothed in darkness, and hold up my arms…

> Please don't give me away—not yet. I'm not ready for anyone else to know I'm dancing in the darkness.

Throwback to Trauma—@ 14 months

It doesn't take much to feel wrenched back to the start of this terrible journey.

We got a new set of baby chicks and were raising them in a box, all downy cuteness and chirping. The yellow one seemed frail and listless and died within a few days. We got a replacement, a fine brown Welsummer chick, which was perky and curious. I went to check on the chicks one morning and found the new one dead, lying on her side, eyes bulging. I burst into sobs, flashing on finding Noah dead, and had to go back to bed.

Another vulnerable creature in my home suddenly gone. Me finding it, Bryan away and not reachable. The same frozen, astonished eyes. An echo of the same shock in my crushed heart, the same guilt for not checking sooner (to adjust the heat lamp), the same not knowing. Here it was again in miniature: the same agitation, heaving gut, hyper-vigilance. The same triggering, seeing everything through the lens of loss.

No more replacement chicks, I told Bryan. No more delicate, dead creatures in my home. I can't stand the risk. I can't look at it philosophically right now as part of the circle of life.

Our hens have been a comfort in the past year as they cluck and peck their way around the yard and come running for snacks on teetering dinosaur feet. I know the new chicks will delight us once they're older and sturdier. When we, too, are sturdier, we can resume tending the circle.

Trauma in the Body: EMDR Therapy— @ 1 month and 16 months

A month after Noah's death, I sat down in a therapist's office and cried my way through the story of his suicide nonstop for two hours with my eyes closed. I poured out my agony in a torrent of tears and shouts, from the unraveling of my closeness with Noah to opening the garage door. I'd never cried like that before, tried to tell the whole story, or given full vent to self-blame. I had to keep putting aside the sweat-covered electronic buzzers in my hands in order to blow my nose; my pile of used tissues filled the wastebasket. Eventually, I sensed the buzzing stop and heard the calm voice of the therapist telling me to breathe deep, lock away disturbing thoughts, and summon my healing colors. Behind my eyes came slow bursts of lavender, swaths of spring green. My stomach unclenched, heartbeat quieted. Afterwards, I scur-ried to the bathroom and peed a torrent as copious as my tears. I felt depleted and shaky, but lighter. Luckily, a friend was waiting to hug me and drive me home.

So it went for my first set of EMDR (Eye Movement Desensitization and Reprocessing) treatments, a mind-body approach that mental health professionals typically use to treat post-traumatic stress disorder (PTSD). EMDR involves alternately stimulating each side of the brain with eyes following the movement of lights from a machine, coordinated with electronic buzzers alternately vibrating in each hand or hands tapping each side of the body—all while focusing on traumatic thoughts and learning to replace disturbing images with healing ones. The idea is to reprogram how we process painful thoughts and memories.

Since that early treatment, I've tried traditional talk therapy but it seems to bypass emotion rather than help me dredge it up. Trauma roots deep in the body, beyond words. So it's no surprise that mind-body approaches may have a more direct effect after traumatic loss. EMDR pried me open, grabbed my gut, let it howl, then put me back together. Hard as it was, that was what I needed.

I sought out EMDR again at 16 months, when overwhelmed with guilt and anger that I couldn't face alone. This time, I found not just release but revelation. When the therapist asked where the anger sat in my body and what substance it resembled, I said in my heart and mud; she talked me through expelling it down through my body and out the soles of my feet. Though I didn't feel rid of the sludge, I felt lighter with the permission to imagine it gone. Till that moment, I hadn't known I felt so contaminated.

Once, when thoughts of forgiveness were blocked, the therapist turned off the flashing lights and had me move between two chairs in a role play. "What would you like to say to Noah?" she asked. "And what would he like to tell you?"

The very idea set me bawling. As myself, I could barely form the words: "Noah, I'm sorry, I didn't see, I didn't know, I wasn't there for you when you needed me." Switching seats as Noah, I collapsed again and croaked, "It's OK, Mom. I know you loved me, I loved you, too." My body heaved with the effort of bringing my dead son to life. "I'm sorry," I said as Noah. "I just couldn't stand the pain anymore."

That session left me drained for days but also reassured: My child was sorry. My child loved me. And I could talk with him whenever I chose to do so.

"Be sure to walk around the block before you get in your car," the therapist reminded me after every EMDR session. I had to walk way more than a block to recover my grip on the ground—in the direction of an ice cream shop!

TO MY FELLOW SURVIVORS:
EMDR is intense, but so is the pain we carry from suicide loss. EMDR and other mind-body treatments may help propel you forward to the next stage in your grief journey. You can read about EMDR online and check websites of therapists in your area to see if they are trained in the method and offer short-term treatments as part of their practice.

Breathless—@ 18 months

Breathless

When grief seizes you,
it roars through, sucks up
your breath like a tornado,
spits you out
gasping
on bare ground.

You strain to recapture
your troubled inhale.
Like the ring on a carousel,
you keep missing it, choking
on bitterness. Like your lost one

you are stalled between worlds, banished
from the flow. You wait
for the wild wind to retreat,
the debris to settle.

Air seeps in at last—
smell, sound, light—
the forward press of time.

The ring lands
in your hand. You
grasp it, hold on.

I've thought a lot about breath since Noah snuffed out his. Crying fits leave me breathless, while yoga and meditation help me to slow and circulate the breath. Focusing on breathing helps me to stop and be present to my feelings in the moment. Giving myself time with my breath and finding the physical space to breathe deeply is restorative, reminding me of the life force and power within.

We survivors need to let the tears out. But we also need to nurture the flow of breath within us if we are to find a way through the pain.

When the Body Still Says No—@ 35 months

I'm well past the shock of early grief, that "involuntary" reaction that feels out of control. "Over time," say Jordan and Baugher (2016), "you may have noticed that your grief has become more 'voluntary.' You probably are becoming much more skilled at choosing when you allow yourself to react to your loss, and when you choose to avoid it" (p. 85). I've noticed that for a while now, the relief of being able to "dose" my grief and tears rather than having them flood me and rule me.

But the body knows what time of year it is. Each year for the past three years in the weeks approaching Noah's death anniversary, I get a dull pain deep in my abdomen, a pinch on my insides. Is it the womb that once held Noah crying out?

Is it my kidneys unable to process the toxins of his suicide? The hurt at the center of my being becomes a constant reminder— of love and unspeakable loss, but also of the need to be gentle with my wounded self at this season. Each year, I ache for my suffering son and the memory of those final weeks that we didn't know were the end. Each year, doctors find no obvious cause and gradually, the pain subsides.

The body still says no, sometimes when I least expect it. Meanwhile, I've come out of the kitchen and found a dance class that feels freeing. I throw a fierce punch in the air as we stomp to the chorus of Rachel Platten's (2015) "Fight Song."

TO MY FELLOW SURVIVORS:
Does your body say no? Are you listening? What are you doing to give yourself the extra care and attention you need in the face of shock and grief?

Visualizing Your Safe Space

When we're traumatized, it's helpful to train our minds to go to a safe space. Think of a real or imagined place where you feel completely at ease, nurtured, held. Maybe it's a magical spot you once visited, something you dreamed, or a special corner of your home. (For me, it's the stream by our cabin in the woods.) Make a portrait of this place in your mind with the details of what you see, hear, smell, touch, and feel there. Let it imprint on your memory. (It helped me to take photos of the place, even a video where I can hear the stream rushing.) When you feel overcome with grief or troubling memories and you need to transition from grief work back to daily life, pause, close your eyes, and summon up that safe space in your mind. Linger as long as you like; you can return there anytime.

Adapted from preparation exercises for EMDR,
a therapy developed by Francine Shapiro, PhD

Chapter 3

WHAT THEY SAY AND DON'T SAY
Dealing with Others

You deserve a caring community of supportive people to wrap you in the cradle of unconditional love and support. You deserve companions who will walk beside you and provide you with divine momentum—affirmations that what you are doing is right and necessary for you and will lead to your eventual healing.

Alan Wolfelt (2009)

10 Ways to Help the Family after a Suicide—@ 3 months

Though our family has received lots of emotional and practical support since Noah's death, there are many who say that "there are no words" or "I don't know how to help." In fact, there *are* words and actions that comfort. I'd like to suggest a few based on what's been helpful to me or what I wish people would say or do. It's not a comprehensive list and of course, it depends on the situation and your closeness to the grieving person after suicide. Some of these ideas could be helpful to families who've lost a child by other means or to those who've lost other family members to other forms of trauma:

1. Don't ignore the elephant in the room. Continue to tell us you are sorry and wish us strength. Mention the dead person's name freely.

2. Leave something nourishing like a loaf of homemade bread or a colorful plant on the doorstep.

3. Ask us, "What are you doing to take care of yourself?"

4. Don't wait for us to tell you what we need; we may not know or be able to say.

5. Bring us calming oils, lotions, herbs, and stones or a relaxation CD.

6. Ask to see pictures of the dead person. Ask if we feel like talking about him today. If you didn't know him well, try, "Tell me more about…"

7. Mourn with us. Sit quietly next to us and hold our hand or hug us while we cry.

8. Give us a book on grieving or a memoir of suicide loss with a personal note.

9. Ask what our day or week has been like. Ask how we feel being back at work or other routines. Don't assume that we're feeling better just because we're back.

10. Tell us about a beautiful place not far away that soothes the soul; offer to take us there when we're ready.

"Lower Your Expectations of Others"—@ 4 months

The literature for suicide survivors tells us to lower our expectations of other people's response to our pain and accept that what they say or do is what they're able to offer. We're told that if we can accept this, we won't be so easily disappointed. Everyone grieves in their own way and on their own timetable—yes, yes, of course. But I still feel dismayed, even furious, at silence.

A friend advised me to visit relatives with zero expectations, and I tried. I played along with the usual joking around; I probably appeared normal. Later, I realized how much strain I'd been under with all that smiling small talk. No one asked how I was feeling, unless questions about work are code for that. No one shared a memory of Noah even in passing, although Bryan and I signaled it was OK to talk about it by mentioning him several times. When we made a toast at dinner, "to Noah, who should have been here with us and who we all love and miss," there was an awkward silence after a somber clink of glasses.

It felt as if Noah had never lived and as if the tragedy of his death had never happened. This made me furious. I know I'm supposed to understand other people's need to keep their distance from sorrow and discomfort. I'm supposed to have empathy for their not knowing what to say. But we survivors are the chief mourners. Why should we have to worry about other people's needs? Why don't they show more concern with *our* needs?

It takes a lot of energy to figure out my needs, maybe because they're in such flux. In the early weeks, I needed to have someone around every day who could listen to and comfort me. And I needed to unburden myself several times a week with major, 25-tissue crying fits, after which I needed to hold someone.

Lately, it's enough if I can freely express my grief with a few trusted people. I don't need to burden every social encounter with talking about Noah, his death, and our grief. I can be grateful for the precious people who welcome talking about it but I don't have to resent those who cannot. Maybe I got frustrated with the relatives because it had been too long since having one of those precious talks. Instead of zero expectations, I had zero tolerance.

Or maybe having zero expectations of others is asking too much of suicide survivors. We should be able to own all the conflicted feelings that come along with this unpredictable journey, including anger and frustration with others' reactions.

(Grief expert Shep Jeffreys [2011] says the bereaved may never get the support we need from some people. Their personal "denial system" is threatened by contact with grief, much less suicide. "We flee the horror of tragic circumstances that remind us of what could happen to us," he writes. Especially with the loss of a child, "others may need to keep away lest contact with the bereaved parent brings up one's own fears of shattered assumptions about the world" [pp. 45, 327]. I'm eternally grateful, then, to anyone brave enough to face our grief and show that they care.)

"I can't imagine what you're going through"—@ 11 months

How often survivors hear well-meaning folks say that they can't imagine what it's like to lose someone to suicide, especially a child. They're trying to convey sympathy, sensitivity, and respect for the enormity of our loss. They don't want to presume what it's like, in part because it's too painful or uncomfortable. They stop themselves from imagining without realizing that their statement can stop conversation and make survivors feel even more isolated and alone—the "other" that no one can truly understand.

It's similar to when people tell us that "there are no words" for this experience. They want to show caring and their sense that words are inadequate to the situation. But the effect can also be silencing. What if we as survivors need to summon words to tell our story and ask our questions, again and again?

Veterans often hear the same lines from non-military folks about their combat experience, I was surprised to learn from novelist Paul Klay (2014), and it sets up a barrier. "You don't honor someone by telling them, 'I can never imagine what you've been through,'" he writes. "Instead, listen to their story and try to imagine being in it, no matter how hard or uncomfortable that feels."

I believe people who say they can't imagine my experience as a survivor of suicide loss. But I, too, would rather that they follow up with a question or a request to hear about whatever I feel able to share. Just as Klay says Americans need to hear veterans' stories to gain a fuller understanding of war, people need to hear survivors' stories to better grasp suicide and mental illness. These are not "other people's problems"; even if these issues have not directly affected someone's life, that could change in a moment.

I started my blog (and this book) for these very reasons: so others could begin to imagine the experience of suicide loss; so I could speak and be heard and connect to fellow survivors; and to break the silence when words feel inadequate. I need to make this experience understandable to myself and others. I often struggle to find the right words. But searching for and voicing them gives me courage as I walk the mourner's path.

What They Say and Don't Say—@ 13 months

At the one-year mark, I'm less needy than I used to be. I no longer obsess over my expectations of others and my disappointment with them. But I still get upset when relatives come to the house, see pictures and scrapbooks of Noah in full view, hear our passing references to him, and say nothing. There's no acknowledgement of how they miss Noah, no inquiry as to how we're doing with the death anniversary. It's as if our son's life and the hell we've been going through never existed. I'm tempted to leave the room.

Recently, a family member made a remark that stung. Drawing a comparison to other young people who were struggling, the person said, "At least X didn't pull a Noah." What?! Is this the only way Noah's name will be invoked, as a poster child warning of what not to do? Will he be remembered by the relatives only for his suicide and not for, say, his wacky humor or his attachment to his grandparents? I was too shocked to tell this person how much it hurt.

There's a 'Bereaved Parent's Wish List' of unclear origins that circulates at grief support groups, like those of Compassionate Friends (Collins, n.d.). Though it's not specific to suicide loss, it reminds me of the wish lists I made in the early months on how others could help us. I'm most struck at this stage by the wish to have others speak the dead child's name, to understand that recovery after this type of loss can be a lifelong process, and of course, the wish that can never be: "I wish my child hadn't died. I wish I had him back."

Remembering Hurts, Forgetting Kindness—@ 32 months

At a family reunion, there were two new blows to add to the list. When Bryan said something about losing Noah, a young father nodded and said it had been a very hard year for his family; they'd had to end a pregnancy for medical reasons. Was he equating the abortion of a fetus to the loss of a child we'd raised and loved for 21 years? I was incredulous. Later, I felt guilty for minimizing his loss in my mind. Everyone is consumed by the enormity of their own pain, and there's no hierarchy of grief.

Another relative I'd only met once before hadn't known that I was the mother of the Noah who had killed himself. "You may not believe this," she began as she launched into a long, tipsy story, "but when I heard about the suicide, I was actually jealous because at least you know where your child is. Mine has a lot of problems and we're estranged." This mother has no idea what it's like to see your child being lowered into the ground in a box and know that the only place to visit him is a cemetery. But then, I have no idea what it's like to deal with a string of crises and the complete cut-off of communication with a living adult child. When we're hurting, each of us lives in our own private hell.

I shared these remarks with my support group, knowing they'd understand. The facilitator asked if anyone at the reunion had shown sensitivity and concern. Yes, I said, my sister-in-law gave me a sweet photo of four-year-old Noah kissing me, and a couple people asked how we were managing. Why do I forget the kindness of others and focus on the slights? Why is it so easy to feel like a victim and an outsider?

I'm not alone in feeling hurt by others' responses to my child's suicide. A study of parent survivors found that harmful responses had been received from family members (53%) and non-kin (32%); about half reported ongoing strained relationships (Feigelman, 2008). The researchers saw these results as indicators of stigma around suicide that persists in our society, though in more subtle forms than in the past.

Hurtful remarks re-open the wound and remind me that I'm still broken, shamed, and isolated by suicide loss, even as I rebuild my life. They also remind me that if I'm learning anything, it's to try to bring compassion to a world of suffering—and to stop long enough to be grateful for the good I've received.

TO MY FELLOW SURVIVORS:
What do you wish others would say or do, or not say and not do? Which items from your personal wish list do you wish you could post on your front door or on your Facebook page for all to see?

Self-Compassion Break

When we feel frustrated or hurt by how others respond to our loss, we can try to give ourselves the care and holding we need by focusing on compassion for ourselves. Psychologist Dr. Kristin Neff offers an accessible, three-part mindfulness practice called the Self-Compassion Break. She suggests that you begin by thinking about a situation that distresses you and noticing how it feels in your body. Then say the following to yourself:

- "This is a moment of suffering," mindfully acknowledging the pain you're feeling.

- "Suffering is a part of life," tuning into the "common humanity" that you share with others so you don't feel alone.

- "May I be kind to myself," putting your hands on your heart and setting an intention to practice self-compassion and forgiveness.

Adapted from Dr. Kristen Neff's (2015)
"Self-Compassion Break" meditation

Chapter 4

THE UNFINISHED PUZZLE

Why and What-If?

I was beginning to see that there was never going to be a straightforward sentence: He did it because... It was all going to be fragments, a snarl... All these bits would keep coming, and that's all they would ever be, bits. Nobody knew the whole of it.

Joan Wickersham (2008)

Rewriting the Script—@ 2 weeks

What if I could rewind the tape and rewrite the script for that fateful Tuesday afternoon? My mind leaps at the prospect, the first good thought in days.

The beginning is the same: I come home from work at 5pm; no Noah. I text him; no answer. I go outside to see if he's taken the bike or motorcycle.

Before I reach the garage, Lobo barks and something catches my eye in the corner of the backyard. It's Noah stretched out on the chaise longue, crying silently. I rush over and kneel by the chair to hug him; he sobs in my arms. "I tried to do it but I couldn't," he heaves. I don't know what he's talking about till he gestures to the rope coiled at his feet. Then I start crying. Frantic, I call Bryan. I smooth back Noah's hair and kiss his head, over and over. I tell him, "We love you. It won't always be like this. Please let us take you to the hospital, please." He doesn't respond. His face looks haunted and shell-shocked.

Bryan gets home, comes running. We're all sobbing now. Bryan and I stand Noah up between us and steer him inside. We lay him down on the sofa in the den. I bring him hot cocoa and sit beside him, stroking his hair. His eyes are closed, tears seeping. My psychologist cousin comes over and talks to him in low tones in private for a long time. "He'll go," she finally announces.

At the hospital, they bring Noah a sedative and ask him lots of questions. He calms down, sleeps, eventually gets seen by a young male psychiatrist. He tells the doctor everything and lets us talk to him.

Noah agrees to start treatment. He sticks to it and it works. His decline of the past two years is gradually reversed, like a movie in slow-motion rewind. He lets us love him and help him heal. He wants to see friends, travel, finish college. He smiles and laughs again, plays with the dog again. We get our boy back from the brink.

This is the closest to a dream I've had about Noah since he killed himself. Replaying this vision in my mind brings a rush of relief for a moment before I remember: It's only a dream.

Piecing Together the Puzzle—@ 3 months

"What do you hope to gain from that?" some people ask when we say we're still struggling with why Noah killed himself. It's not about gaining something but needing to know as much as we can about our child and his mental state now that he can no longer speak for himself. Bryan and I will never fully understand what happened, but we know more now than we did three months ago. There are fewer missing pieces of the puzzle, even if the outline of the overall pattern is still murky. This comes from talking with Noah's therapists and friends; reading his writings; and looking at documents like medical records and the coroner's report—all massive invasions of privacy that would never happen in the normal course of a young adult's life.

Each new bit of information can be unsettling: Noah's rejection of medication, his dread of more anxiety attacks, his and his buddies' belief that they were "bulletproof" after a friend's suicide. His desperation is evident in writings a year before his suicide, seemingly in response to an anxiety attack: *How far can I fall and still climb back up? Who's going to catch me next time? My greatest fear is to wake up one day at the bottom and find I haven't fallen but have been descending step by step.* Later, when back at college, he wrote: *Cocaine, ecstasy, no homework / Mom, I do drugs / Thought twice and said yes both times / Tell one lie I dare you.* In the scattered, mostly undated writings, it's hard to separate Noah's words from the words of others, fact from fantasy, Noah's journal from his notes for characters in screenplays. In his last weeks at college, he aggressively pursued a young woman who kept rejecting him (and whose friends likewise rejected him, maybe even bullied him); did this push him over the top?

Some people turn their backs on detective work after a suicide, feeling that "what's done is done—it won't change anything." But the search for clues has given us glimpses into Noah and his struggle and brought us closer to him. It's let us stitch together a possible story of what happened, based on as much information as we've been able to muster. We couldn't protect our child from his demons but we could dedicate ourselves to this search as the least thing we could do for him—to accompany him through his struggle to the end.

The need to know and to ferret out clues is a common impulse for suicide survivors as part of the grieving process, according to researcher Kari Dyregrov and colleagues (2012). It's OK to leave no stone unturned, they say, as long as this doesn't become a long-term obsession. "Struggle with 'why' it happened until you no longer need to know 'why' or until YOU are satisfied with partial answers," advises Iris Bolton (1987, p. 289), a founder of the suicide loss survivor movement.

Bryan and I met with a psychiatrist for a psychiatric autopsy based on Noah's history. The meeting was gentle and informative, though, of course, not definitive without Noah in the room. The doctor said Noah's symptoms were a puzzling mix that defied a clear diagnosis. We'll never know if he suffered from the onset of bipolar or schizoaffective disorder, beyond his earlier diagnoses of major depression and anxiety disorder. With this, we've come to the end of the road for the moment.

What will we do with our time now? Will we revisit the puzzle years from now and see a fit among the pieces that eludes us today?

(I later came to feel that Noah had untreated PTSD from his own suicide loss. His good friend—a brilliant student and athlete, bubbling with energy, who had a psychiatric history she kept well hidden—killed herself on campus in an especially dramatic way at the start of Noah's sophomore year in college. In the shocked aftermath, Noah and her other friends turned inward and shut out offers of counseling. Noah was the one who got the others out of bed and off to class. He muscled through the school year; his depression didn't fully surface till summer, when he started therapy for the first time. He had a severe anxiety attack upon returning to college around the anniversary of his friend's death, which may have been what prompted him to leave school for a year. We didn't know about that attack or subsequent ones, nor did we know that losing someone to suicide raises the risk of suicidal thoughts. Did his therapists know?)

"He Made His Choice"—@ 4 months

He made his choice, some say.

But an act of desperation is not a choice. A choice is a deliberate decision made after considering the options. The suicide literature says that people who kill themselves are no longer able to see other options; they've lost their problem-solving abilities. Hence, the idea that suicide is a permanent solution to a temporary problem.

Some people with terminal illness, chronic pain, or a degenerative condition make an action plan for suicide when they reach a certain point. I can accept that such people might make a rational choice to take their lives. Their loved ones might even understand their reasoning. I've always assumed those people were unlike Noah because they were usually elderly, had suffered pain for many years, and had no hope of a cure. I didn't see that my son may have had similar reasons to end his life. If he felt his suffering was unbearable, had been going on for a long time, and could never be fixed, then in his mind, maybe it was chronic pain and a degenerative, terminal illness. Maybe he felt he had no option other than to end the pain.

"It hurts me to think how much pain he must have been in to do this," Noah's uncle said in the early weeks. I don't know if I'll ever be able to face my son's pain. That would mean putting myself in his place, which feels too threatening. I want to live a good life and die a natural death. I've never been suicidal.

If we don't know what utter despair feels like, day after day, week after week, with no hope of relief, we may never truly understand someone's need to end it all—and their blindness to other choices.

Precious Life/Tragic Death—@ 7 months

From Lisa Richards' (2012) *Dear Mallory: Letters to a Teenage Girl Who Killed Herself* comes a beautiful dedication that I wish I could feel, much less write: "For Mallory Erin Richards/In Loving Memory/May her precious life and tragic death help guide us toward creating a wiser and more compassionate world for all."

Precious life. Tragic death. I can't hold those two ideas in my mind right now. I get stuck on the "precious" part. Noah's life wasn't precious to him anymore. He didn't cherish it; he destroyed and discarded it, and so much along with it. He either didn't believe his life was precious or didn't care anymore. All our precious love for him, shattered and useless in the face of his despair. Now instead of a life to cherish, there's merely a memory. How do we cherish a memory? Can we love it like a child?

I'm in awe of how Richards' pure, passionate love for her daughter flowed free, even in the months immediately after Mallory's suicide. Richards' letters to Mallory abound with tender, funny memories and quirky descriptions of her child's life and personality. I can barely conjure an image of Noah and rarely flash on memories or feel his presence. The love between us, under such strain the last couple years, is still too troubled to bubble up; with his suicide, it feels blocked.

Tragic death, I know well and feel acutely. How to find my way to Noah's precious life?

When Did the End Begin?—@ 9 months

I've had a hard time with endings since Noah died. When making a scrapbook of his life, I couldn't face writing the year of his death or figuring out what to put on the last page because there shouldn't be a last page to your child's life. Books, movies, TV episodes leave me teary even if they aren't that sad, simply because they're ending. I start to get upset as I sense a story moving toward its close; it reminds me of how we didn't know that our family was moving toward an ending. What we thought was the beginning of Noah getting well was actually the beginning of the end. We thought he was coming home from college to get better; he may have known he was coming home to die.

When did the end begin? When he lost a good friend to suicide and almost lost another to an attempt? When he had his first debilitating anxiety attack and didn't tell us? When friends stopped answering his calls and he stopped smiling? When something else scary happened, maybe drug induced, that we'll never know? Those contemplating suicide have the end in mind, obscuring everything. We survivors—burdened by love, worry, and our own limitations—can't seem to see the end till it's over.

The next few months leading up to the first anniversary of Noah's death will be full of little anniversaries of the steps leading to the end—how he fell apart, how we failed to help or even recognize the full extent of the danger. As I relive each step in our son's decline, I wonder if someone had intervened to change even one thing whether Noah might have been diverted from his path. Instead of those steps leading him to the abyss, they could have led him, no matter how circuitously, back to life.

The mini-anniversaries hurl me back into the pit of what-ifs, could-haves, and should-haves as we move toward the anniversary of an ending.

Chance—@ 18 months

Chance

You took chances.
So many ways you could have died
on surfboard, snowboard, motorcycle—
just one blindsiding wave, curve, car.
I worried, you scoffed, we played
our parts; you stayed intact.

Disasters I conjured
but never this torrent
swamping your soul.

You took no chances.
You could have set it up
to disappear at sea, plunge
off a cliff, but
a rope over the rafters
leaves no mistake,
no clue,
no you.

Death with Dignity v. Death by Suicide—@ 23 months

I'm easily triggered with the second anniversary of Noah's suicide approaching. My tears burst from a full-face grimace. I see a young quadriplegic on TV fighting to regain his strength and growl in protest; why didn't Noah fight for his life? I'm back to fixating on how this did not have to be.

I hear a segment on the radio news about a "good death" and the death with dignity movement. Though I've been a lifelong supporter of death with dignity, I can't hear talk of a good death right now; I'm too close to the worst kind of death.

Death with dignity can ease the pain and passing of a terminally ill person, ideally in the company of family and friends with supportive end-of-life care. Death by suicide ends the pain of the suffering person and passes it on to their family and friends, denying us a chance to help or say goodbye. It forces survivors to look directly into the face of death and despair and to recognize not only our lack of control over the actions of people we love but our limited understanding of their hearts and minds.

Death by suicide does violence to the body of one person and to the soul of many, leaving a trail of destruction and doubt. It puts the health, happiness, and sometimes the lives of survivors at risk. It's a violation of trust with our loved ones, yes, and a tragedy. But it's also a violation of the social and natural order—a small-scale crime against humanity. It scares me to be so blunt, but that's what it amounts to when we consider the collateral damage. No wonder suicide has been so widely forbidden and punished across history and cultures.

I'll always try to understand Noah's suicide and suicide generally. I'll try to be compassionate with those who take their lives and with those who suffer with or without mental illness. I'll continue to join the call for breaking the silence and advancing research and services around mental illness and suicide. But I won't make excuses for my son or others who kill themselves. I miss Noah too much. I hate suicide too much. I'll continue to rail against the violence he did to himself, to everyone who loved him, and to our world.

I trust I won't always feel this way. Our loved ones who died by suicide were not criminals who intended to hurt us; they were lost in terrible pain. But this did not have to be.

The Unfinished Puzzle—@ 33 months

We had a buoying visit this week from one of Noah's friends we'd never met. She was generous with her memories and seemed comfortable talking about Noah, though she said it took her a long time to finally contact us. I'm grateful to her for reaching out and for bringing us little stories of Noah's college years, like how he helped organize an all-night Asian-style dance party and how a group of 15 friends once made a fried chicken dinner in his honor and how he inspired her to take art and music classes that became a solace for her after his death. Also how in his last months at school, he looked and acted different and no longer said hello—and how much that hurt.

I've always felt I owe Noah's friends and cousins an explanation for his suicide. No one asks "why" directly, yet the question hovers over many encounters. What happened to the adventurous, charismatic, affectionate guy who became a husk of his former self? What happened in the three weeks between leaving school and killing himself? His college friends said goodbye to Noah and turned him over to me to take him home and give him the care he needed. He took his life while under my roof in my care. How can that be?

The day after the young woman's visit, I was enjoying a front-row seat at a concert when suddenly the poignant Tchaikovsky melody overwhelmed me and I felt dragged down by the misery and mystery of the last three weeks of Noah's life. We thought he was safe with us at home; we saw him daily, had dinner together. Yet he was far from safe from his demons. He refused to get help and wouldn't let me or anyone take care of him as he sunk deeper into numbness and isolation, ignoring the few friends who called. If only I'd known about his massive anxiety attacks and his dread of having more. If only I'd understood how extreme isolation is a warning sign for suicide and how having lost someone to suicide can be a risk factor. If only I'd brought home Noah's friends or one of several therapists we know, whether Noah wanted to see them or not. The litany of if-onlys in my mind drowned out the beautiful music, each one an accusation.

I could tell Noah's friends and cousins about those three weeks. I could admit how confused, helpless, and angry we felt as parents when Noah wouldn't get help—and they might know exactly what I meant. Because that's how they probably felt, too, during Noah's decline. None of us understood what was happening or what to do.

No matter how survivors shuffle the pieces of the puzzle, there will always be gaps in the picture. We'll never really know what was going on in the mind of the person we thought we knew. As Jordan and Baugher (2016) say, we need to learn to live with the blind spot.

TO MY FELLOW SURVIVORS:
Have you allowed yourself to investigate questions about your loved one's suicide as long as you feel the need? Have you found support on this part of your journey, lest you feel overwhelmed by what-if and if-only?

Containing Disturbing Thoughts

Another practice to deal with trauma is to visualize a container that can hold your most disturbing thoughts and memories to give you a break from them. The container should be something that can be opened and closed like a box, case, trunk, bag, closet, or room. It can be real or imagined, big or small. When beset with disturbing thoughts about your loved one, sit quietly with eyes closed and summon up the container in your mind. Imagine dumping all those thoughts into the container, closing it up, and leaving it aside. The thoughts will still be there if you need to revisit them later but for now, you're giving yourself a much-needed release from their grip on your mind. This technique is most effective when used as part of therapy sessions for processing trauma, like EMDR therapy, but is also recommended by therapists for self-care.

Adapted from preparation exercises for EMDR, a therapy developed by Francine Shapiro, PhD

Chapter 5

FOREVER 21
Birthdays, Anniversaries,
and Memorials

Each anniversary of our loved one's passing is yet another opportunity for us to say good-bye—the farewell we didn't get to say the first time around.

Catherine Greenleaf (2006)

First Birthday—@ 3 months

Noah's birthday came too soon after his death. Yesterday he would have been 22. We should have spent the week preparing for a pool-side BBQ with kebabs, apple pie, and ice cream. Instead, we marked the day without him with moans and tears. We still can't believe there will be no more birthdays for our child.

Bryan visited Noah at the cemetery without me. I don't feel that Noah's spirit is in that horrible box in the ground. It's hard to know how to reach someone who so adamantly did not want to be reached, who violently quashed his spirit without a goodbye. On his birthday, I wanted to try to commune with Noah's spirit at the ocean he loved.

We met my cousins in the late afternoon at a beach in Santa Monica where Noah learned to surf. At once, I was caught up in the power and expanse of the waves. I could call out, "Noah, where are you?" and no one would hear me. Young men in wetsuits were paddling out, all expectation; Noah should have been with them, face to the wind. The surfers mounted their boards, flipped over, tried again, dove under. Why couldn't Noah have treated his troubles like an oncoming wave and scrambled back on board? Scanning the gray horizon, it was all possibility and adventure—or it was all desolation and oblivion. By the end, he could see only the emptiness.

His cousin is convinced that Noah is a dolphin racing the waves, at one with nature. I'm still looking for a sign of Noah's enduring presence in our lives, a sign of how we should mark all the birthdays to come.

This May Be the Last Time: Approaching the One-Year Memorial—@ 11 months

In a few weeks, it will be a year since Noah's suicide. Next week, we'll have a graveside memorial for the "unveiling" of the stone. Time has sped up like a falling meteor with the countdown to this date. I've felt frantic as if preparing for some impending disaster. My sleep and stomach have been haywire, just as they were in the weeks after Noah's death. I was reliving our sense of helplessness as we witnessed his decline and refusal to get help.

A year ago, Bryan and I thought Noah was at the beginning of a time to heal and redirect his life. We had no idea he was so wound up that he felt his clock ticking down. We had no clue that in one rash instant, we'd be robbed of time and son.

Last year, we were too frozen in shock and anguish to be fully present to mark Noah's death. We made hasty choices for his burial and funeral. We couldn't formulate words for a speech. We sequestered ourselves out of sight during the service and rushed away moments after the coffin was lowered. We couldn't believe we were leaving our child in a box in the ground in an alien place.

Since then, we've huddled by Noah's grave under the privacy of a big umbrella, crying and calling out to him or telling him the latest family news. We've chosen his gravestone and fingered the little love objects others have left there. That patch of earth with his name on it has begun to feel familiar. It's still hard to grasp that Noah's not away on a long trip, bound to come home full of presents and stories.

When I was Noah's age, I used to sing a traditional spiritual, "May Be the Last Time":

> *This may be the last time we sing together*
> *Oh, it may be the last time, I don't know.*
> *(Chorus) This may be the last time*
> *This may be the last time, children*
> *This may be the last time*
> *May be the last time, I don't know.*

There was a last time that Noah and I ate together, talked together, walked or cooked together—and I didn't know.

The unveiling will be the last time a group of people gathers at his grave. Our family will say goodbye in a way we couldn't do at the funeral. Bryan and I have been sifting through grief poems, writing a speech, arranging food. We're still wounded. But we're in charge this time. We're not the same family who hobbled away from the grave a year ago as if missing limbs.

Leave-Taking: After the One-Year Memorial—@ 11 months

It's over: another milestone. Maybe you've been there. After so much anticipation, you wake up and it's time to get ready, to drive somewhere, to sit quietly while people gather, then to hold hands with your family and weep while you take in the memorial you've planned. You remember your beloved person in the company of others, one year after the suicide.

Our memorial for Noah is an intimate, homemade ceremony for the unveiling of his gravestone. This return to the grave with 30 friends and relatives is a re-immersion in grief without the raw shock and devastation of the funeral. On this day, as a friend says, we truly bury our son.

With eyes closed, I sense the muffled cries and sniffles around me, the tears of my son, Ben, beside me. I focus on the personal touches that make the day meaningful: jazz music of Avishai Cohen that Noah first heard with his French host family. Haunting Native American flute melodies played by his cousin. The candle lit by his grandfather. The luxuriant red camellias picked from her garden by his grandmother. Covering the gravestone, the frog-design quilt his aunt made for him as a child in a pattern called life cycle. The ever-evocative lines of Psalm 23. Our speech, inspired by the text on his gravestone. The words people call out when asked how they'll remember Noah: *adventurous, inspiring, goofy, loving, wonder*. The stones and shells that each of us place in a snug embrace around the edges of the marker. Some are from Noah's favorite places, like a surf spot; others are from places he surely would have visited had he lived, like his best friend's ancestral home in Italy.

Infused with love on a brilliant sunny day, Noah's marker is beautiful to behold. This grave site will never again be so abundant.

My cup runneth over. The sobbing begins at the end for my husband and me. Our son's life is over. This collective leave-taking is over. We don't want to leave; for us, it will never be over. We linger.

Back home, friends, family, food, flowers—re-entry into the world of the living. The buoying warmth of it.

How will I try to remember Noah? Alive to life's possibilities.

A Memorial Speech for Noah's Family and Friends—@ 11 months

"Today is likely the last time a large group of people will gather to focus on Noah. There will be no birthdays, send-offs or welcome home parties; no graduation, wedding, baby namings, or all the little celebrations of life. Today seems like the time to say a collective goodbye and try to face the fact of his death, carved in stone on this permanent marker.

This is not the mark we ever imagined Noah would make on our family or the world. We'd like to share our thoughts about what is on this stone marker—about Noah's dates, his name, and his gifts.

Noah Chayim ben Benyamin v Shoshana
1991–2013
So many gifts
Much loved, sorely missed

As parents, we gave Noah life—the 1991 on this stone. No parent should live to see the death of their child; certainly no grandparent should live to see the death of their grandchild. It has taken us most of this year to be able to face the painfully compressed dates on this stone, 1991–2013. It's still unbelievable. Noah does not belong in this cemetery that is, as he would have said, 'full of old people.'

As parents, we gave Noah his name: in Hebrew, *Noah Chayim ben Benyamin v Shoshana.* We chose an N-name to honor Bryan's late grandfather and because we liked the sound of Noah. Like the biblical Noah, our Noah was drawn to animals, loved his wine, and spent a lot of time in the water—surfing, sailing, swimming, kayaking, playing water polo, and relaxing with friends in the hot tub. Like his namesake, our Noah was a traveler, often storm tossed and far from home. Tragically, our Noah was not a survivor. The journey was too long and terrifying, the promise of green land too dim and distant. He was swept away in a flood of emotion and confusion, unable to imagine any olive branch or rainbow appearing after the deluge.

We who loved Noah may think he didn't seek shelter soon enough or take heed to build a vessel strong enough to withstand disaster. We may lament his lack of fortitude, foresight, or faith. But unless we have ourselves been caught up in such a storm, we cannot know how hard it was for him to weather it as long as he did. We cannot know how grimly fear, shame, and despair twist the mind.

In another cruel twist, Noah's middle name was Chayim, Hebrew for life. It's hard not to feel that in dying by suicide, Noah rejected life, aborted the journey before takeoff. Yet we have to remember that for most of his 21 years he embraced life with gusto, curiosity, and love. His life was full of adventure and rich with friends and family. As he struggled to grasp what was happening to his mind, maybe he sensed—and could not accept—the possibility of mental illness constraining that life.

The final part of a Hebrew name ties a person to his parents: *ben Benyamin v Shoshana* (son of Bryan and Susan). Noah cherished being part of a large, loving extended family, and he had a soft spot for his Jewish cultural roots. As parents, we felt fortunate that he stayed close to us longer than most adolescent boys and that he actually wanted to spend time with us discussing ideas, eating out, watching films, backpacking, or juggling. With all his beauty and promise, all his struggle and complications, he will always be our precious younger son, bound to us in love.

So many gifts. As parents, we gave Noah some of the many gifts and opportunities he received; so, too, did his brother, grandparents, cousins, aunts, uncles, good friends, lovers, teachers, and mentors over the years. How lucky Noah was to have and develop a strong body, sharp mind, tender soul, sly wit, artist's eye.

And there were the gifts he shared with others: his passion for friends; his infectious courage and *joie de vivre*; his omelets and pizzas and tarts; his listening when others were sad or lost; his endless questions and conversation. 'Noah was a man who made things happen,' a college friend of his wrote. 'It is heartbreaking to imagine all that he might have made happen—buildings designed, films directed, images created, friends touched, women and children loved.'

We have learned a lot about Noah and his struggles in the last year, though we will never fully understand what happened. By the end, it seems, he no longer believed in the gifts he had to offer or felt the love that surrounded him. He didn't know that his death would leave so many people feeling not only shocked and saddened but, quite simply, robbed.

As we move into a second year without Noah, we pray for the wisdom to know how to cherish his memory and restore our lives."

First "Deathaversary": The Solace of Memories—@ 12 months

I like fellow survivor Charlotte Maya's (2014) term "deatha-versary," used to separate this date from happy anniversaries, with its reminder of how "averse" we are to having to mark such an untimely death.

We made it through a year, the first one without Noah. The actual day wasn't much more upsetting than many other days leading up to it. That may change in future years when we're less focused on grief and the date seizes us without warning.

As with other special dates, it helped to have a plan. We planned to go to Noah's favorite surf spot and walk the beach path, then visit his favorite taco place. It was a glorious spring day, sun glinting on the tips of the waves and the shoulders of the surfers. They surfaced at a distance like a pack of seals. I could almost picture Noah among them, paddling out with his long torso leaning out over the board.

It brought back a raft of memories to be in that parking lot again where I brought Noah so many times before he could drive. His constant check of the online surf reports. His loading up on donuts early in the morning. His eagerness to get to the water. The rip in the arm of his wetsuit. His cool nods to the more experienced surfers while covertly watching their moves. His turning back to shore one morning, thankfully, in a fog so dense I lost sight of him within seconds. Old hippies on the sand in Santa hats at Christmas. I used to wonder if Noah would become one of those grizzled old guys who never stop surfing.

It took being at the beach to recover those memories. I rushed to write them down for fear of losing them. Unlike other family memories, they can never be recalled with Noah himself in some relaxed moment.

This first deathaversary brought gifts: The many kind cards and e-mails. The realization that, as with my father, I don't need to carry Noah's pain in order to love and cherish him. The readiness to make some travel plans. The recently widowed friend who said there are no rules in grief other than to be gentle with yourself.

The most precious gift was an e-mail with a story we'd never heard from one of Noah's friends, who is Chinese. He told how on a visit to New York City, Noah was the only friend willing to go with him to an obscure dim sum dive in Queens and eat a dish of tripe and pancreas without a grimace, just a quick reach for his teacup. That image made me smile on a sad day.

Anything that adds to the impoverished storehouse of memory is a comfort, even a thrill—as if Noah were here telling the story himself.

Second Birthday—@ 15 months

On Noah's birthday, I think, we should go places and do things that he loved, like seeing the new Wes Anderson movie or having dinner at his favorite gourmet pizza place. We should let ourselves imagine what life would have been like if he'd lived and recovered.

I imagine Noah as a 23-year-old college graduate, having made that cross-country drive he always wanted to do, working a summer job as a photographer's assistant for a movie shoot, out every night but sure to be home for his birthday BBQ with family. I see him chasing the dog and the chickens, playing chess with his dad, maybe consenting to talk with me if I caught him at the right moment. Seizing on simple pleasures, trying to find his way.

If only we had a normal life to celebrate with normal ups and downs and a healthy son joking around at the table. Or even a suffering son smiling weakly, letting us love and help him as he sought calmer waters.

The second birthday was difficult, maybe because we didn't have a plan for the day and didn't tell those around us what we wanted. It was hard to be with our son, Ben, who doesn't like to "talk about sad things," and other relatives, who didn't acknowledge the date. Bryan needed to retreat from socializing. I worried that it might hurt Ben to turn a short visit with him into mourning time for his brother.

The next day, Ben agreed to watch some family videos together. I reminded him of when he and Noah were sitting on the rumbling Paris Metro, far from Bryan and me, laughing and bonding after years of teenage estrangement. I said how sorry I was that he'd miss out on more brotherly times together, and we both cried. Then we were riveted by video Bryan found of interviews he did with Noah around age 13, which none of us had ever seen. Noah's voice and face were changing; he had a new seriousness and was starting to sound like his older self. I was so entranced to see my dead child talking that I only absorbed bits of what he was saying, like what he thought he'd be like ten years from that time: "I don't know but I know I'm going to be listening to jazz."

Later, Bryan and I set aside our grieving selves to enjoy time with Ben and his girlfriend. Figuring out how to love both our sons with one foot in both their worlds.

Second Deathaversary—@ 24 months

How bad can this day be when I've been grieving intensely for a week, feeling the dreaded countdown to March 19?

A few days ago while Bryan was away, I took out the folder of Noah's writings that I hadn't touched in two years and that I'd only read while still in shock after his death. The folder felt radioactive; I considered not opening it. But I was determined to revisit his writings in the hope of finding some new piece of the puzzle or new place for the pieces I already had.

The writings were much as I remembered them, still chilling, still mysterious. There, again, was part of a Brian Eno song about no longer being able to read between the lines, mixed in with Noah's own jottings. There, again, the signs of Noah's loneliness and despair: *In a cocoon in a crowded room / Terminally disenchanted / When did the fog roll in?* I found no great revelations in the re-reading, despite knowing more now about Noah's mental health and about suicide and mental health conditions generally. The writings reinforced the story I already knew and reminded me of some strands I tend to overlook, like possible drug abuse or psychotic reaction to drugs. I'll return to this folder all my life and try to understand the mind that wrote these disturbed jottings.

I told my therapist that it hadn't been too emotional to revisit Noah's writings. But as soon as we started using the buzzers in my hands for EMDR treatment to physically process the feelings (see Chapter 2, Trauma in the Body), I wept nonstop, sensing the depth of Noah's pain and his fear of losing his mind. *O brain/ Brain mush*, he wrote sometime in his last months or weeks of college. I hadn't touched those thoughts for a while or fully admitted them while re-reading his writings. I felt shaky and disoriented for hours.

The next day, I let body and soul rest. I went to see a friend who's making me a memorial bracelet and suddenly felt hopeful and cared for, fingering the charms we've chosen to represent Noah's life that I'll soon carry with me everywhere (see Chapter 9, Memorial Bracelet).

Third Birthday—@ 27 months

Birthday

On your 24th birthday
I wander the house, kissing
your head in every photo.
Only cool glass grazes my lips.

From your closet I grab
a zip-locked pack of T-shirts
sealed with your scent. I open it fast
and breathe you in, still thick
with thrift-store musk smoke sweat.
I ration these releases
to last a lifetime.

We walk along the beach where you
used to surf, where we used to scan
the waves for your lean, concave form.

But you paddled out too far, dropped
over the horizon. Now we see
only other people's sons,
their brave bodies braced against
the ocean's pull.

Driving home under mottled clouds,
a rare smudge of rainbow—
an afterthought.

The gold-rimmed evening sky stunned me on the way home from the beach. Maybe on future birthdays, we should think about gifts: the ones Noah had, the ones we gave him and he gave us, the ones we would have continued to exchange had we been given the gift of time.

Third Deathaversary—@ 36 months

Dear Noah:

Your third deathaversary is one of simple moments and magical thinking. We get donuts from the shop where you used to beg fresh ones in the middle of the night. We look through digital photos so Dad can post one on Facebook in your memory. I pick an old-fashioned photo album at random—1995—and immerse myself in your four-year-old cuteness. I'm struck by your soft, tentative gesture and pensive expression looking down at a baby tortoise, much as you looked years later holding a kitten. You communed so deeply with animals.

So when a friend tells me she believes our souls live on in others, I wonder if "others" can mean animals. And if that's what was happening in the last photo we have of you when you smiled as you looked down at our new dog, Lobo—a real smile like we hadn't seen in months. An uncanny gold light rises from your shoulders in the photo as if you'd been touched with a blessing. Was that the moment when you gave over your spirit to Lobo, knowing he'd be our solace after your death?

We bring jasmine and roses to lighten the heaviness of your stone at the Children's Memorial Garden. Your ex-girlfriend joins us, handing us a beautiful card. We sit with her and another friend at a café in the old neighborhood, lingering on a sunny afternoon. There's a toast to you and reminiscences; no one at this table is afraid to say your name. Later, we stroll through a California native garden just coming awake with blooming lupine and poppies. We feel soothed; the day isn't as hard as we feared.

The next morning, we're surprised and touched by a Facebook post from Ben, who's traveling in Nepal. His gloved hand holds up your driver's license in front of snowy Himalayan peaks: "Remembering Noah in a place he would have loved." The best thing in our day!

We have a tradition now to ease ourselves back into life after marking your death: a trip to that little central coast beach town you showed us that we've come to love. We slow down, breathe deep, fill ourselves with ocean smells and sounds. We watch Lobo frolic in the froth and bound after sandpipers. I write hearts in the sand for you and gaze out at the water, hoping for a whiff of your presence.

In a photo from your teenage years, you're sitting in the breakfast nook, grimacing as you stretch your long arms out as wide as you can to try to touch both walls; you nearly do. I picture you laughing at me now with my mystical wish. You stretch your arms out impossibly wide over the ocean, hovering there, as if to touch the edges of it. *See, Mom, I'm here, OK?*

"We can always dream," says Dad. "What have we got to lose?"

You are in your dog's foolish heart. You are in the vastness of things I'll never understand.

Two days after your anniversary comes the spring equinox.

Love,

Mom

TO MY FELLOW SURVIVORS:

How are you navigating the triggering days? I hope you have companions in grief who can share your journey and help you find activities and personal rituals that feel right.

Grief Collage

As your loved one's birthday or death anniversary approaches, try a healing creative activity pioneered by survivor and art therapist Sharon Strouse. In *Artful Grief: A Diary of Healing*, Strouse (2013) recounts her grief journey and describes how she used collage to express her anguish and memorialize her teenage daughter. Her workshops for survivors exhibit and discuss some of Strouse's remarkable poster-size collages, then offer materials for collage making and a process to debrief each other's creations. You'll need thick paper or cardboard as backing, a glue stick, and magazines with evocative images and words (Strouse suggests tearing these out rather than cutting them). A cheap source of old magazines is your local library bookstore or thrift shops. You can see what images strike you or search with a particular theme in mind. Be free and play; there are no rules. When finished, you may want to journal about your collage or share it with a friend.

Adapted from Sharon Strouse's workshop on Artful Grief

Chapter 6

LIVING THE NIGHTMARE
Parenting and Family Life

We parents can only give our children our humanness, which means our positive qualities along with our negative qualities... [W]hat a child does with our parenting is his own choice. His life is his responsibility.

Iris Bolton (1983)

We Lose More than Our Future—@ 3 months

When you lose a child, you lose your future.

We parent survivors lose the sweetness of projecting our child's life into the future: the joy they would have brought to our lives with their friends and romances and accomplishments and adventures; the life cycle celebrations we would have treasured; the new people they would have brought into our families to love; the chance to live vicariously through them as their lives expanded and ours contracted; our comfort in old age. We lose the possibility of passing some of who we are on to the next generation—our little hold on immortality.

When we lose a child before they've had a chance to mature, we lose out on seeing them become their adult selves and find their place in the world. We lose out on the culmination of our parenting, which was to launch them as independent adults ready to enjoy and engage in life and contribute to the world. Their suicide aborts the launch and implies they didn't feel equipped or inclined for the journey, calling our parenting into question.

While grappling with the enormity of this truth, we also lose our present. We lose entire weeks or months while our bodies and psyches absorb the shock of suicide. We lose our grounding in the things we loved or believed or thought we understood. And we lose the little moments we shared with our child that we took for granted but would give anything to recapture now: a homemade breakfast, a quick phone call, a smile.

And we lose the past, with family memories overshadowed by a violent, unnecessary death. How can we look at pictures of happier times when all we can think of is how it wasn't meant to end this way? How can we be grateful for the years we had with our child when there will be no more years with him or her?

We're suspended in time without the future, present, or past we thought we had.

First Family Vacation—@ 4 months

Another first in the first year after Noah's death full of firsts: first family vacation without him. It was good to get away from all the immediate reminders of his death at home. I could relax some of the time, though it felt strange devoting the days to pure enjoyment after all that mourning. It was good to spend a week with our son, Ben; his company cushioned Bryan and me from the pain that might have engulfed us traveling alone.

Every day but one, I thought and wrote about Noah and cried. He should have been on one of the sailboats bobbing in the lake, charging ahead of us up the mountain trail, or taking sunset photos. He should have been joking with his cousin, talking motorcycles with his uncle, dissing me with his brother. He should have been gorging on seafood, berry pies, and plate-size pancakes. He should have been using his blue duffel bag, not us.

I had photos of Noah in my purse so I could bring him with us on this trip. I took them out in my moments alone and showed him the wilderness beach. *All the places you could have gone, the things you could have done. The person you could have been, if you'd only given yourself a chance to heal and grow up.* I resolved to take him with me when I travel and bring him where he can no longer bring himself.

Wandering down the beach, I found myself drawing in the sand with a piece of driftwood as tall as my shoulder. I started with a heart, then wrote Noah's name inside it, facing toward the sea. *I'll write your name on every beach.* Feeling our way, creating new traditions...

What I Gave—@ 5 months

I gave Noah my all—everything I had, everything I knew. All the fun of singing and stories, teddy bear picnics and snake-themed birthday parties. All the appreciation of art, languages, world events. All the ways of understanding and being with others. Strong cultural roots with the freedom to explore beyond. More love than I knew I had. I poured so much of it into this child, maybe because he was so receptive from an early age, so eager to engage in years-long conversation.

I gave him my all and it wasn't enough. It didn't prepare him for the tumult of young adulthood or protect him from his demons.

Of course, I wasn't the only hand shaping him, nor would I want to be. So much that we can't fathom intervenes between the formation of a child's cells and a parent's attempt to shape his character, between the years of nurturing and the years when our children break away.

I imparted many values to my children, from the political to the personal, but it never occurred to me that I needed to reinforce the life force. I thought the value and richness of life was self-evident. I thought self-preservation was human instinct.

We give our children life and love and all the opportunities we can muster. When they throw it all away in a moment, we lose not only our child and our hopes. We lose our life project as parents, our faith in what we have to give.

So Much Sorrow, So Much Love—@ 5 months

The first few months after losing Noah, I was overcome with how much sorrow there is in the world. It was as if I'd suddenly sprung an antenna tuned to signals I hadn't noticed before. Sorrow flooded in full force from all directions, just as simple happiness had once filled me in pregnancy and early motherhood. Awash in the universals of death or birth, there's no filter to the sentiment or sentimentality connecting us to others.

So many ways to lose a child. The hand-wringing helplessness of losing babies and young children to disease before they can even enjoy their childhood. Anguish at the randomness of losing kids to violence or accident. The living losses that can last for years, like losing teens to addiction, anorexia, or depression, or losing adult children in faraway places to family estrangement. And especially, losing family members to serious mental illness, struggling to keep them safe and healthy while subsisting on remnants of relationship. I'll never know if that might have been our family's lot, too, trying to banish the demons that had taken over Noah's mind, praying they were only temporary.

I was going through this litany of loss while walking with a friend whose brother has lived for decades with schizophrenia. I was about to say how much sorrow there is in the world when my friend said, "I know, there's so much love in the world." She reminded me of the surrogate brothers who had blessed her life, of the many people who stepped up to support us since Noah's death, of the ways families keep hoping for healing.

To sense only a world of sorrows is to think like Noah may have done, tuning out a world of love. There were so many people who loved our son and hoped to reconnect with him when his troubles eased. When laid low with pain, we need to leave ourselves open to those sustaining springs.

NO—@ 13 months

Survivors all have triggers we can't avoid. I've heard of grief waves set off by the cereal aisle in the supermarket, a favorite piece of clothing, a bridge on a crowded freeway. For me lately, it's billboard ads for the epic disaster movie, *Noah*. *No*, I think as I drive past the ads on my way to a lunch appointment, *I don't want to think about that right now*. This sends me down a rabbit hole of *no*'s and hurtles me back into the poetry writing I've been avoiding for a year.

No

Noah—his name
blaring from movie billboards,
signs of disaster
at every turn. No
reminders please.

His name engraved
on a stone, rain collecting
inside the O's. No—

my screams
that day—not
my beautiful boy. No

knowing why or how.
Mission aborted,
family broken. No

more
please—just the sweet no's
we sang him as a baby—

When the No-no-noah goes bob-bob-bobbing along.

Craving the Ordinary—@ 11 months

I find myself wishing for ordinary things. To eat a simple meal with my child and hear about his day. To see him going out with friends or roughing up the dog. To greet him as he comes toward me in the airport after a trip. To kiss the top of his head. What I wouldn't give to relive such moments.

My mother raised me to strive for the extraordinary, and I passed that on to my kids. Noah felt pressured to be a unique person with an unusual life. Maybe he didn't realize that he'd be loved regardless of his accomplishments. We didn't realize that his despair was far out of the ordinary, that his most extraordinary act would be one of self-destruction, and that the most distinctive thing about our family life would be this tragedy. I'd trade that for the ordinary anytime.

I hear co-workers talk about having their grown kids home for dinner and watching TV together or taking the dog to the park. I see parents with their young adult children eating out, going to a movie. I want to grab them and say: "You're so lucky. You get to sit down to spaghetti with your child, even if they're moody or on their cell phone. Cherish that time."

I'm getting used to the crushing fact that the only anniversary we'll ever share with Noah is the anniversary of his death. I still can't believe we'll be forever deprived even of those ordinary moments we once took for granted.

More Than—@ 16 months

Noah was more than a person who took his life.
His biography is about more than its ending.
I am more than the parent of a child who killed himself.
My parenting is about more than failing to save my child.

I thrash my way to the surface, up through the muck of labels and stigma, refusing to let suicide swamp my life force or overshadow memories of my child. If all these things are "more than," then there's much to salvage: more memories, more relationship, more parts of myself that have been on hold since the suicide.

My life as a mother shouldn't be defined by or minimized by having lost a child to suicide. Yet this is hard to believe in my bones. I've heard that a newborn's DNA crosses the placenta into the mother, so it's not just sentimental for biological moms to feel that our lost children live on within us or that a part of ourselves has died with them. (Or for other parents to share that powerful emotion.) How can we be more than our dead children's struggles when we're so enmeshed with them?

My parental identity feels fragile as eggshell, everything I did to raise this child now laden with doubt. I start to advise a friend on how she could cut down on thrice-daily phone calls with her daughter at college and I have to catch myself: I'm disqualified now from that sort of talk. I need to step back and listen and learn all I can. I need to focus on being a good parent with Ben, including letting him move through this sad time in his own way.

It's the shaming, crippling impact of suicide loss on the sense of self as a parent that I've thought, written, and read least about, maybe because it's so threatening. Those of us who've lost a child to suicide embody every parent's worst nightmare; who wants to look that in the face?

Psychologist John Jordan (2011) observes that suicide survivors:

> usually overestimate their own power to influence or control the events that led to the suicide and are unaware of, or underestimate, all the other elements that contributed to the death. They also frequently make the cognitive error of evaluating their actions before the suicide in light of what they have come to know after the suicide. (p. 198)

Might parent survivors need to fully express our doubts and regrets before we can accept our limitations and embrace what it means to be "more than" parents of a child who killed himself?

Dreaming Your Name—@ 17 months

Dreaming Your Name

The name we gave you
we dreamed to see
on a diploma,
a wedding invitation—
maybe someday

in photo bylines
or film credits.
We could picture it
on a Brooklyn doorbell
a far-flung postcard
a note of reconciliation.
Never
on a stone.
Never forever
unreachable
in the favorites
on my phone.

Families and Final Acts—@ 21 months

I was relaxing with the Saturday newspaper, reading columnist Chris Erskine (2014) muse nostalgic about an old black and white photo of a family Thanksgiving. I was pleasantly buoyed along on his twisted wit till I fell on a passage that made me wail and throw down the paper. These photos, he wrote, "remind us that families falter but are rarely finished. There may be bad moments, challenges, moral decay, deceit, tough love, belly laughs, hissy fits, spit-takes, boozy fights, gossip and grudges that never go away. But there are no final acts."

But wait, I want to say—there are children and others who lose their way, far from family's embrace or a vision of the future. Numb to love, they abandon us and commit the ultimate final act. Suicide blasts all that solid rock of family to dust.

I'm reminded again how survivors are banished from normalcy, sidelined from simple truths. We can no longer assume there will always be family. So much that others take for granted as universal no longer applies.

How we need that "community of comfort" of fellow survivors at support groups and other gatherings to normalize our experience at holiday time and any time. We don't know these people like family; until a final act, we may have had little in common. Now we greet each other along the mourner's path.

We tell our stories, hug, and cry. We cheer each other's steps in the hard climb out of the hole.

When Couples Grieve: Apart and Together—@ 22 months

The hole that a child's death blasts through a family can tear a marriage apart. Friends reminded Bryan and me of this when we snapped at each other in the days after Noah's death. The anger, guilt, and remorse surrounding suicide loss compound the risk of lashing out at or withdrawing from one's partner. This brought Bryan and me to couples therapy for a while and still resurfaces.

How can someone who's suffering such a grievous loss comfort a partner who's suffering the same thing? In the early months, Bryan and I didn't have much comfort to spare; we were too depleted. We cried alone and confided in precious friends, cousins, support groups, therapists. If we reached out to the other during a crying fit, we were both in tears and struggling for calm. We clung to each other at night, awake in separate nightmares. "We had the same injury and different symptoms," as O'Rourke (2011, p. 104) observes of other grieving family members after her mother died. My husband and I were doing parallel grief, like children do parallel play.

I'd rarely seen my husband cry before. For weeks after Noah died, several times a day, he sobbed and rocked on a bench in the backyard. I'd never seen his good-humored face so crumpled, his eyes so cloudy, his shoulders so defeated. His features were stricken for months, then settled into an unfamiliar glumness. I felt terrible for him who had never had a major loss before. I wished I could enfold him in a soft cocoon and that he could do the same for me.

I worried that if I was upset and Bryan was numb, any lament from me would catapult him back into misery. Or if I was feeling steady and didn't realize that he was teary, whatever I did might jar his mood. It was hard to know from one moment to the next whether we could grieve together or grope our way out together, whether we needed time alone or with others. Like many couples, we struggled with how much space to give the other before it became a chasm. Only this was even more confusing while in a blur of pain.

It's one thing to say people grieve differently and another to live it every day with your spouse in a broken family. One of us took a leave from work; the other went back after two weeks. One of us became immersed in reading and writing related to suicide; the other in gardening, home improvement, and hobbies. One of us promptly left social gatherings when uncomfortable; the other felt obliged to be present. One of us found Noah dead and couldn't go in the garage for many months; the other felt at home there because it was the last place Noah had been. Sometimes one of us, sometimes the other, could relax and enjoy a little.

We came together over comfort food, comfort TV, Shabbat services at our synagogue, and visits with Ben. We shared inspiration from our respective support groups and frustration from gatherings with relatives who avoided saying Noah's name. We teamed up to arrange psychological autopsies and track down every clue we could find to our son's demise. We planned memorials and Noah's birthday and agonized over what to put on his gravestone.

Gradually, we began to remember Noah together. We brought each other stray memories and pictures like gifts. We treasured every message and visit from Noah's friends.

Now almost two years after the suicide, we're on firmer ground. We can usually tell if the other is having a grief surge and offer a hug. We can bring up anything to do with Noah without worrying that the other is not ready to hear it; his life and death are so much on our minds that any mention, anytime, seems natural.

We still grieve differently. Jordan (2011) calls couples' differences in grief "coping asynchrony" and points to a common contrast between more "instrumental" approaches to grief that are action oriented versus more "intuitive" approaches that focus on the outpouring of feeling. These two approaches exist along a continuum, with many people blending them along their grief journey (Jeffreys, 2011). Guess which way I and many women lean?

I delve into the whys and what-ifs of Noah's situation and of suicide generally; my husband doesn't want more information. He visits the cemetery regularly to talk to Noah and give him the latest news; I mostly avoid the place. I want to travel to refresh my mind and carry on Noah's wanderlust; my husband feels safer at home. Grieving as a couple is sustaining—I know it would be tougher on my own—but also constraining. Whatever else, we know each other better for walking this path, alone and together.

TO MY FELLOW PARENT SURVIVORS
WITHOUT PARTNERS:
I think of you and hope you've found others who can accompany you as you move through this journey.

When Couples Grieve: Traveling in Different Directions—@ 28 months

Bryan and I never made it to Glacier National Park in Montana. Our three-week road trip from Los Angeles turned into two weeks. We traveled with differently weighted grief packs taking up more and more space in the car. I was eager to see new vistas in the Northwest and explore the route together like we had on a fun cross-country trip the year before Noah's decline. Bryan, tied to home as steadying comfort, was anxious being away. Little things sparked panic; normal pleasures felt flat. "Do you want to turn around?" I kept asking, but he said we should continue.

Then in an unfamiliar town, our dog, Lobo, disappeared into the woods at dusk and didn't come to our calls. He finally turned up half an hour later but not before turning Bryan ashen at the fear of another loss. We managed to have a good hike the next day with friends—and Lobo firmly on leash. I knew something was still wrong when Bryan refrained from climbing a higher peak from the overlook, as he often does. The next day, he left the farmer's market after a few minutes without even tasting the local apricots. This time, we decided to cut the trip short.

On the long drive home, Bryan seemed relieved to be heading back to the familiar. I was glad for his sake but worried whether we'd ever be able to enjoy traveling together again for more than a few days. Once home, we reveled in the tomatoes and peaches that had ripened in our absence. Then I caught a glimpse of our shrine to Noah in the dining room and my heart collapsed. *Back to this again; still here, still dead.* The reminders of Noah that fill our home are what I need to leave behind for fresh perspective—and what my husband needs to hold close for security and comfort. I look forward to the novelty of travel; my husband is wary of feeling unmoored. A support group facilitator tells me this kind of divergence is common for survivor couples.

After stewing in some glumness of my own, I'm trying to see the shortened trip as a blessing, forcing me to journey inward with creative pursuits this summer. Slowly, my husband and I are debriefing what happened and seeking things other than travel to look forward to together.

When Young Adult Siblings Grieve—@ 34 months

Since Noah's suicide, everyone has been asking how his brother, Ben, is doing. It's been hard to know with Ben living in another city and not inclined to talk much about his feelings. Of course, he was in shock and distress at the funeral, letting loose a terrible cry when the coffin was opened. He had brief outbursts of sadness at the one-year memorial, cemetery visits, and no doubt other moments that we as parents didn't see. Though he rarely talked about Noah or grief, he called and visited us often in the early months and listened to us talk and cry; that was his way of accompanying our grief journey. He didn't (and still doesn't) want to attend a support group, see a therapist, or talk to friends about his loss.

Ben was almost 24 when he lost his brother. He seemed determined to not let tragedy cloud his cheerful disposition or derail the life he was building with a new job, a girlfriend, and a great apartment in San Francisco. "I was on a roll and I didn't want anything to stop me," he later said. He went ahead with a birthday party that his girlfriend had planned shortly after the funeral and said it was comforting to have his friends around him. While I didn't want him to be overwhelmed with grief, I didn't want him to act as if nothing had happened. I wanted him to be part of our family's grief journey. I've had to learn to accept that his different way of grieving is a common response for young people after suicide loss, especially young men. I'm just afraid one day grief will hit him full force and we won't be there to help him.

It pains me that Ben has trouble remembering the good times growing up with his little brother. Noah adored Ben as a child, following his lead in making forts and dams and obstacle courses for the dog. Our boys moved in different worlds as teenagers and weren't close as young adults, though they were starting to spend more time together. Ben told us he wished he'd reached out more to Noah. He and I share regret about things not said and done and the forever lost chance at reconciliation.

Our super tall sons had started to look more alike as adults. After Noah was gone, we'd sometimes be startled at the resemblance when we glimpsed Ben in profile or at a distance. He began to wear his beard like Noah, his pant legs rolled up like Noah. He said Noah inspired him to be more adventurous and irresponsible. He began rock climbing. He quit his job to travel for a year. He brought back a bottle of sake from Japan and poured it over Noah's grave. He said he wished they could have traveled together—how if Noah had arrived with him after hours at a castle in Spain, Noah would have scaled the walls to check it out. Maybe the new roads that travel opens up will give Ben space to grieve and remember.

I'm glad Ben thinks about Noah as he explores the world. I'm so sorry he can't explore along with Noah, much less do the ordinary things adult brothers do like go out for a beer, throw a Frisbee, or make fun of their parents. Bryan and I never meant for Ben to be an only child. As he seeks his path, I hope he finds brotherhood with others and an enduring bond with Noah's spirit. Wherever he ventures, Noah would surely cheer him on.

(When Ben came home after a year of traveling, he showed Bryan and me a video he'd made. There, to our amazement, was a flickering succession of travel scenes with Ben's hand holding up Noah's driver's license in the foreground of each shot—174 scenes in all, set to pulsating music. "I wanted you to know that I was thinking of Noah," he said. I watched, transfixed and teary. It wasn't just that Noah will never see the Moroccan desert, Thai beaches, or Himalayan Mountains where his photo ID now has been. It was that Ben must have had his brother in his heart on at least 174 occasions to create this video.)

Ben's gloved hand with Noah's driver's license, Nepal, 2016.

Letter to a Mourning Mom Who Blames Herself—@ 35 months

Dear Mourning Mom of 10 months:

I know you. I was you in the first year or two, and sometimes still in bursts of remorse today. I hear your cries of all you should-have, could-have done for your lost child. This is how we often feel as survivors, especially parent survivors.

We think we failed our child and we need to shout out our unworthiness, beat our breast. On top of the general stigma of suicide, we may be afflicted by the special shame of being a bad mother—one who couldn't foresee or prevent her child's self-destruction. Instinctively, we reject assurances that we did everything we could because, of course, there's always more we could have done. Even when people add "given what you knew at the time," we just can't accept that we were unable to save our child. That the momentum of our mothering only goes so far with our kids. And that, unlike other parents, we don't get a second chance.

Having missed that chance, we cling desperately to remorse as a last parental act. It keeps us connected to our dead child. It shows our love and loyalty and belated understanding of what they needed and what we failed to provide. It's a desperate plea for their forgiveness. Except that now, only we can forgive ourselves. And that could be a long time coming.

You have a total right to feel whatever you're feeling. By all means, let it out! At the same time, please feed your battered soul. Treat yourself with the same compassion you would offer a dear friend in your position. Make a list of all the great things you did for and with your child over the years. Remember that no one is a perfect parent; no one is all seeing or all powerful.

"Just as no one can erase the grief that you feel right now, there were limits to what anyone could have done to fix your loved one's pain," according to Jordan and Baugher (2016, pp. 9–10). "Living through the suicide of a loved one confronts all survivors with a profound sense of their own limitations" (p. 10). You may feel like putting yourself on trial for failing your child, they write, but at least let someone like a therapist ensure that it's a "fair trial" that reviews all the evidence.

I know you can't fully take in what I'm saying right now. Please tuck it away in the back of your mind to ease some future moment, along with these words from psychotherapist Stacey Freedenthal (2014):

Feelings of self-blame can distract you from grieving and, in the process, from healing... What lies beneath your self-blame are the terrible facts that you cannot control: Suicidal forces overtook your loved one. You have suffered an unfathomable loss. You cannot turn back time, do it over, do it differently. Each of these is a loss. Mourning these losses is the essence of grief. Your grief deserves your compassion.

TO MY FELLOW SURVIVORS:
How has losing a family member to suicide changed your view of family life and your place in it? If you're a parent survivor and feel like you've been living the nightmare, what are you doing to put yourself back together in the morning? Have you left a way open to rebuild your identity as a mom or dad?

Dialogue Writing

You may have written about your grief in a journal or in a letter to your lost one, but have you tried writing a dialogue with them? "All suicides are unfinished conversations," Lesoine and Chöphel point out in their helpful book, *Unfinished Conversation: Healing from Suicide and Loss* (2013):

> There is so much that we, the living, still need to say and want to hear from those who take their own lives, leaving us with no opportunity to communicate... Write an interactive dialogue between you and your deceased loved one. You might begin with a simple conversation about the kinds of things you used to talk about... When you feel ready, let your conversation go deeper... Explore the disappointment, frustration, anger and pain you both feel. Listen beneath the suffering to hear and say what you're each really trying to communicate. Whatever had been said or left unsaid, done or left undone, express it through ongoing interactive conversations. (pp. 4, 52)

Chapter 7

GRIEF HOLIDAY
Hallmark Occasions

Grief requires acquainting yourself with the world again and again; each 'first' causes a break that must be reset… [M]y mother's death was not a single event, but a whole series of events—the first Easter without her; the first wedding anniversary without her… The lesson lay in the empty chair at the dinner table. It was learned night after night, day after day. And so you always feel suspense, a queer dread—you never know what occasion will break the loss freshly open.

Meghan O'Rourke (2011)

Avoiding Halloween—@ 7 months

Ten years ago, I scouted out weird Halloween displays in front yards to show my kids. Our strobe-lit front porch had giant spiders, skeletons, Day of the Dead ornaments, unearthly didgeridoo music, and hundreds of trick-or-treaters.

This October when I walk in my neighborhood, I'm assaulted with ghoulish images that are someone else's idea of fun. I'm surrounded with effigies hanging from trees, a daily reminder of images I'm trying hard to forget.

When I found Noah hanging in the garage, the scene was so macabre that I thought it was an effigy of him someone had strung up for a prank. I couldn't believe he'd done this violence to himself. For weeks, I was haunted by details of the scene (see Chapter 1, The First Horrific Days). I wonder if anyone who has seen a loved one hanging can ever look dispassionately on a hanging scene at Halloween, much less in a movie or photograph. I still can't face looking at rope or even the word "rope." These things are my enemies, doorways to the nightmare.

I didn't count Halloween on the list of tough holidays I anticipated this year. But the profusion of hanging figures, open coffins, and RIP gravestones disturb my peace. There's no resting in peace for people who kill themselves and the ones they leave behind. Every day is a day of the dead for survivors. Every triggering effigy, another sign that I'm walking the mourner's path at a great distance from the everyday.

Flight Response—@ 8 months

I used to think of myself as someone who faced adversity and would rather confront the truth than hide from it. Since Noah's suicide, I've been running from many things, unable to face certain symbols, rituals, dates.

I fled from the prospect of an open funeral. *No, no, only the family, please.* The cantor of our synagogue gently convinced us that having the community present could be a comfort and that we could sit in a private space during the ceremony.

I cringed at the thought of going to Shabbat services, my raw grief exposed. "Just come for the last ten minutes, say the mourner's prayer, and leave," urged the rabbi. We did that for weeks until we could sit for longer periods and face the music— literally—without collapsing.

As Noah's birthday loomed closer, I wanted to shut out the world. *Make a plan for the days you dread,* I'd heard. I planned to have a scrapbook of his life ready for the day, go to the beach with my cousins, and make pizza with them like Noah used to do. It was a hard day but better than hiding.

For Thanksgiving, I longed to escape to another country or take a road trip to the desert, far from home and reminders of Thanksgivings past. *Connect with those you love on holidays,* I read on grief handouts in support groups. Slowly, we began inviting guests and planning the menu. We're still talking about how we'll make a toast to Noah's memory and ask for what we need.

Each time, what I most feared turned out to be what I most needed.

Thanksgiving: Grief Holiday?—@ 8 months

This Thanksgiving, our first big home holiday without Noah, was suffused with sadness, unknowns, and ambivalence. How to make room for sorrow at the celebratory table without burdening everyone?

Bryan and I ended up hosting dinner for ten. It wasn't ideal, but it was better than being alone or having other hosts set the tone. We went through the usual motions of shopping, cooking, laying the table, and greeting guests, only we needed more rest than usual. After much deliberation, we came up with a short speech noting our distance from gratitude this year as we feel the pain of Noah's absence. We lit a Mediterranean blue candle in Noah's memory to evoke his love of the ocean, of France and Italy, and of good food. Everyone readily joined in a toast to Noah's life, as if relieved to show support. Then we sat back and let a few lively talkers give the meal a festive air. I was getting through the day by rote with some moments of pleasant distraction; Bryan was unusually quiet. Sleep fell heavy that night as we crossed from a noisy, normal, peopled space back to our own lonely planet.

Survivors are supposed to allow ourselves grief holidays, designated time out from grief. Rather than a grief holiday on such occasions, maybe some of us need a reprieve from the holidays so we can retreat into our private griefworld.

Next Thanksgiving, we'll know not to host. Mourners should be able to appear or disappear at will, free of any expectations or responsibilities.

Catherine Greenleaf (2006) offers this advice to survivors on anticipating holidays: "We can balance our busy times with quiet, conscious reflection…whatever brings us back to our center. Then when we start obsessing about the missing person at the Thanksgiving table, we can draw on those reserves of serenity" (December 13).

Letting the Light Go Out—@ 9 months

'Tis the season of light linking winter solstice, Christmas, Chanukah, and New Year. We did a candle meditation in front of the Chanukah menorah at my Jewish meditation group. What should have been calming and inspiring was agitating and I had to leave the room. I couldn't focus on tending the flame of our inner light. All I could think of was my two boys at a school holiday program years ago, earnestly singing about not letting the light go out in Peter, Paul, and Mary's stirring "Light One Candle."

Noah's light was gone now, snuffed out by his own hand. In truth, his light went out some time before as depression overtook him and wiped out all feeling or connection.

Noah's photography professor told us how passionate he was in her class a few months before his death, how she would look up from lecturing to see his face glowing. Somehow that class reignited him; his flame rallied. I wish I could have witnessed that last firing up of my son's spirit.

I want to tell the loved ones of depressed people everywhere not to let the light go out. Be alarmed; don't hold back out of deference to the person's privacy or autonomy. Intervene before they are too far gone to be reached.

"We are holding Noah in the light," Quaker friends wrote after Noah's death. I tried to hold him in the light with prayer and healing energy while he was suffering. It's hard to summon light around the thought of my child in a box in the ground.

The days will be getting longer now. Will we survivors be ready to let in more light as time passes? To tend the flame both of our loved one's memory and of our own lives?

New Year Intentions—@ 9 months

I've been wishing people happy new year half-heartedly, as if from a distance. I'm operating on another calendar in an alternate universe. I'm attuned to the end of the first year since Noah's death in three months. When I think of 2013 ending, I think of the engagement calendars I'm saving: his, with its entries that stopped in the spring, and mine, with its stark reminders of funeral arrangements, doctor appointments, and visits from Noah's friends.

I want to send words of hope for a better year to my fellow survivors and all who are struggling. What might help parent survivors is "moments of intentional remembering, cherishing the gift of our child's life and love," writes Janie Cook (2013). And for mourners grappling with the extra stress of the holiday season and having trouble with the notion of gratitude, a teaching from Rabbi Yael Levy (2013):

> Let's set an intention to treat ourselves and each other with care and, when faced with the question, "What am I thankful for?," let's notice the sensations and emotions that arise. And when gratitude feels beyond our grasp, let's say to ourselves and each other:
>
> I am present to…the sadness in my heart. I notice…that this has been a difficult time.
>
> I am aware of…the grief I am feeling. I acknowledge…my struggles and the struggles of those around me.
>
> In the new year, may we set an intention for remembrance and be present with whatever is in our hearts.

Graveside Valentine—@ 11 months

Who knew Valentine's Day could be so hard? I always gave my kids little hand-cut hearts, candies, and other silly trifles. This year, I texted my son, Ben, a virtual valentine. I knew I'd need to go to the cemetery to give Noah his.

I thought the cemetery would be full of mourners with valentines on February 14, but it was empty. I'd only been there once since the gravestone was installed; I was still getting used to that little square of earth as our place to commune with Noah. I marveled at the little things left at the edges of the marker: seashells, earbuds, a bronze Class of 2009 decal, half-smoked cigarettes with lighter, plastic solar-powered flowers. It was comforting to see signs that others had been there. I brought an envelope of pink paper hearts with "Mom" on the back, which I staked out around the grave with toothpicks. Thus festooned, the marker looked suddenly festive.

I wanted to shower Noah with the love I should have showered him with in his time of need. He had cut himself off from me in the last two years of his life, put a wedge between us much like Jill Bialosky's (2011) sister did to hide her desperate mental state from the person who knew her best. I was waiting for an opening from Noah, not realizing it was I who needed to open my heart. In his last, low weeks, I should have told him every day that I loved him, that it gets better with help and time. Instead, I showed my love by pushing him to see a psychiatrist. I blew him a kiss the night before he killed himself. I'm left with the crushing sense that my son died without a mother's love.

Suicide makes those left behind doubt our love. We wonder whether our lost ones felt our love or truly loved us. Over and over, we retrace the missed chances to show our love and fling it out like a lifeline. Over and over, we see but can't accept that our love wasn't enough to save our loved ones or keep them close.

When someone is terminally ill with physical illness, we can keep vigil, declare our love, and try to mend old hurts as we say goodbye. When someone is in distress, possibly mentally ill, and secretly planning to end their life, there's no chance for loving farewells. How differently we might have loved had we known.

A Mother's Day Gift from Strangers—@ 14 months

Mother's Day felt blessedly full this year compared to the bleakness of last year. We rode bikes to meet my in-laws for breakfast; I tried not to look at all the intact families with young men around us at the café. On the way home, we passed the house where our boys were born. I took a bubble bath, read the Sunday paper, and had a leisurely phone call with Ben. Bryan surprised me with a card he wrote on behalf of Noah, "what I wish he could have written to you." That evening, we hosted our book group for the first time since Noah died. For most of the day, I felt grateful to be present in the onward flow of life and connected to others.

I didn't seek out time to grieve that day, but it came the moment I stepped into the Children's Memorial and Healing Garden in a quiet corner of a park in our old neighborhood. There are many such gardens around the country created by religious institutions, nonprofits, or individuals, but we'd never heard of our local one until recently. There's an arched gateway made of willow branches at each end of a small, shaded grove. A stone path winds past mosaics and inscriptions, a sculpture of children at play, and boulders marked with the names of lost children. I immediately felt at home and sheltered. Here was a spot dedicated to remembrance, set apart from yet surrounded by the activity of the park. What a gift to grieving families, and how fitting to finally see it on Mother's Day. I immediately wanted to add Noah's name to the garden and imagined visiting him there rather than the cemetery.

As I left the garden, I noticed these reassuring words engraved underfoot:

> *From frustration, sadness, depression, and fear,*
> *To the joy of remembrance, lightness and cheer,*
> *All emotions are welcome here.*

Thank you to the strangers who made this sanctuary—an unexpected gift this Mother's Day.

Ordinary Holidays—@ 43 months

It's almost back-to-ordinary holidays. This Halloween, I peek with curiosity at some of the extravagant yard displays in our neighborhood rather than averting my eyes. This Thanksgiving as we make plans, we're fretting more about traffic and who will do the after-dinner clean-up than about whether we'll cry at the table.

New traditions are settling in. I light the candle by Noah's photograph before the holiday meal. Bryan brings little pumpkins, turkey figures, and other tokens of the day to Noah's grave while filling him in on the latest news. This is no longer heart-rending; it's just how we move through the year.

Mother's Day and Father's Day, Noah's birthday and death anniversary will always be hard. Meanwhile, we're back to sharing the rest of the calendar with the world.

TO MY FELLOW SURVIVORS:

Do you have a plan for how you'll get through the next holiday? Or maybe a new tradition you and others can create this year in memory of your loved one? What little gestures, symbols, or rituals will keep you feeling connected to your loved one on holidays?

Guided Meditation: Finding Gratitude amidst Grief

I created this guided meditation for a winter holiday gathering of more than 100 people sponsored by Survivors after Suicide of Didi Hirsch Mental Health Services, inspired in part by Beyond Loss support group facilitator Mary Wallace. The meditation can be done alone or with a group. You may want to audio record it or have someone read it aloud softly and slowly, pausing between each line, while you try it.

Close your eyes and sit quietly... Feel your feet on the floor and your body in the chair with your hands resting in your lap... Slow down your breath and breathe in gently for a count of three...then out for a count of three... Breathing in this moment...breathing out any distractions... Maybe breathing in a blessing in your life...breathing out gratitude for even one small blessing... Breathing in...and out...[long pause] Now take a moment to bring to mind the love you shared with the person or persons you lost...[long pause] As you think of this, place your right hand over your heart, breathing in that love...and breathing out...breathing in to let that love fill you...and let it out...[long pause] Now think about someone or something that has supported you on your grief journey... With that thought, bring your left hand on top of your right hand that is still resting on your heart... Breathing in the possibility of gratitude, now or in the future...and breathing out... Breathing in the wish to open the heart...and breathing out...[long pause] Relax as you continue to focus on your breath and the warmth of your heart... When you are ready, open your eyes.

Chapter 8

"WHO SHALL LIVE AND WHO SHALL DIE"
Spirituality and the Jewish Year

Give me the gift of remembering... Shelter me with the gift of tears... Strengthen me with the gift of hope. May I always believe in the beauty of life, the power of goodness, the right to joy.

Rabbinical Assembly, Yizkor Memorial Service (1998)

The Limits of Compassion—@ 5 months

For two years as Noah struggled with depression and anxiety, I prayed that he be blessed with *rachamim* (compassion) for himself, along with *shalom* (peace) and especially *shlemut* (healing or wholeness). Now that he's gone, I pray for all these things for myself, my family, and Noah's friends. Compassion feels like an accessible door to the much more complicated place of forgiveness.

I feel compassion for Noah's terrible suffering. He was likely too overwhelmed by pain to see another way out; I know I shouldn't blame him for this. But I'm still too hurt and angry. I used to love to chant the line on Shabbat: "God, the soul you have given me is pure." Now I feel tainted, bursting with the impurities of bitterness, remorse, self-pity. I can't yet find a pure, open-hearted compassion for my child, maybe because I can't find it for myself.

One day while meditating, I sense a light behind my closed eyes in the shape of hands cupping a human heart. Why couldn't Noah cherish his tender soul? How can I gently hold my own vulnerability and imperfection in the light as I grieve?

"Who Shall Live and Who Shall Die": Fearing the Jewish High Holidays—@ 5 months

I used to approach the High Holidays with appreciation for the tradition of life review, repentance, and celebration. But this is not a normal year. I don't need the *shofar* (ram's horn) as a wake-up call to remembrance and reassessment or a month of preparation for pouring out my soul; I've been doing that daily since Noah took his life. This year, I cringe at the thought of every intense, soul-searching theme of the holidays. How can I have a "sweet year" when there's a brand new memorial plaque in the synagogue for our 21-year-old son?

May you be inscribed in the Book of Life. So say the prayers and greeting cards for Rosh Hashanah. The *Unetaneh Tokef* prayer, always solemn, now feels threatening:

> On Rosh Hashanah it is written, and on Yom Kippur it is sealed…who shall live and who shall die, who shall live out the limit of his days and who shall not, who shall perish by fire and who by water…who will be at rest and who will wander…who shall be at peace and who shall be tormented… But penitence, prayer and good deeds can annul the severity of the decree. (Telushkin, 1991, p. 565)

My ancestors recognized the presence of tormented souls and wandering Jews, though they failed to include "who by their own hand" in the accounting of ways to die. Where is it written that a beautiful young man full of promise had to reach the end of his days before they'd barely begun? Noah's death was not part of any divine plan or the result of wrong-doing. And no amount of atonement can reduce the severity of this loss.

We raised our son to embrace the Book of Life but somehow, on the verge of a new chapter, Noah lost hold of the binding—

to loved ones, the life force, and his own tender soul. We didn't know that he was no longer on the same page of assuming that life would go on. The best I can do this year is to pray that everyone who loved Noah, especially the young people, reaffirm our place in the Book of Life and our ties to one another.

My rabbi says just let the High Holidays wash over me. My support group buddies say that anticipation of a holiday is often worse than the day itself and the important thing is to have a plan for how to spend it. They all remind me to be open to the healing power of ritual and community.

Past a Fearful Gate: After the High Holidays—@ 7 months

I was dreading the High Holidays last month, especially Yom Kippur, the Day of Atonement. It was painful at times, yet bearable and even a little calming.

On the Jewish New Year in synagogue, instead of singing, I listened to the wall of sound that rose around me. I felt lifted up by other voices that would carry the tune for Bryan and me, even if we couldn't join in words of gratitude. Good friends sitting behind us said they had our backs. People we barely knew came up to wish us, with special emphasis, a *good* year.

On Yom Kippur, we were lucky to have Ben visiting as a hedge against the intensity of the day. I took in the sight of Noah's new memorial plaque fairly calmly, though ordering it and trying to tell my mother-in-law about it had left me mute with grief. Bryan was overcome to be standing at services as a family of three instead of four. He turned to me at one point and said he was about to cry; I thought he'd walk out to take some time alone. When he started sobbing and shaking, I hugged him hard and pulled his prayer shawl over his head for privacy, then ducked under the tent of it to cry with him. Soon Ben was embracing us and crying, too. It happened again during the Yizkor memorial service. The three of us clung to each other and wept while the rabbi read the names of those who had died in the past year; even my cheerful mother-in-law was tearful.

It was OK to cry; we were in a sanctuary. Later in the darkening space as candles were lit to mark the end of the holiday, we sang, swaying arm-in-arm with a row of relatives. We smiled to see Ben on the altar join in a long, final blast on the *shofar* (ram's horn), like he did when he was ten. We'd passed through another fearful gate on our grief journey and come out battered but safe.

I've always loved the harvest holiday of Sukkot, which follows Yom Kippur. For years, our family built the traditional three-sided *sukkah* (harvest hut) in our backyard, decked its top with palm fronds, and hung it with fruit, greenery, and popcorn chains. When our boys were little, they, their friends, and our dog ran endlessly around the *sukkah* while the adults ate and drank inside it. Now, I hoped someone would invite us to their *sukkah* before the holiday was over. Amazingly, someone did, and I felt a fleeting sense of peace after dinner under the harvest moon. I only wish that Bryan and I could have, as the prayer says, "spread a *sukkah* of peace" over Noah and that he could have found the peace he needed to persevere.

Blessing a Child's Journey—@ 7 months

This week's Torah portion from Genesis 12:1 begins with God's call to Abraham to "go forth from your land, your birthplace, your father's house, to the land that I will show you." The song interpretation of this passage by Debbie Friedman and Sabina Teubal, "L'chi Lach (Go forth)," about going forth and being blessed on one's journey, has always moved me.

Noah embarked on a lot of adventurous journeys in his life, from wilderness trips at age 13 to a year in France at age 17 to a challenging college far from home, and we cheered him from the sidelines. He knew he had our blessing for finding his own way in his own time, though he blamed himself for not being focused on one definite direction like the high-powered high achievers he assumed were all around him. Maybe I was so intent on encouraging his exploration that I didn't do enough to reassure him that he would always have safe harbor at home.

How I wish he could have felt blessed on his journey and lived long enough to find his own sense of God or self-compassion.

How I wish that we were not on this grim journey after Noah put an end to his. It's hard right now to see his life as a blessing.

What Prepared You for This?—@ 10 months

I read about an Orthodox man in Israel who, upon hearing that his son had been killed in combat, immediately thanked God for the 19 wonderful years he had with his son. Rabbi Sharon Brous commented that this father's years of religious observance had prepared him well to deal with tragedy, not to remove his pain but to have the strength to see a way forward (Comins, 2010).

I'm in awe of this father's ready response of gratitude. Even now, ten months after Noah's suicide, I'm too hurt to feel grateful for the 21 years we had with him. And I resist the idea that people are only given as much sorrow as we can bear, as if Noah had somehow calculated: *My mom is strong. She's been through this before. She'll be OK.*

What prepared me for this journey? Nothing and everything. Nothing prepared me for the shock and sorrow that still feel like a knife in the gut. If I don't think about the pain too much, I can almost forget it's there; then I have a stray thought and it sears again.

We call on everything and everyone we have after a loved one's suicide. What I call on comes mainly from almost 40 years of mourning and attempts in recent years to nurture a spiritual practice.

I lost my mother to cancer when I was 19, my father to suicide when I was 26, and a close friend to cancer when I was 40. I often felt like I lived in a separate, walled space—a mourning grove—that most people were afraid to enter when they lost someone. I tried to open the gate for others, show them around the griefworld, and assuage their fears. Had I not already spent so much time mourning—even had I not studied Greek lament and mourning traditions in my twenties—how much more lost and afraid I might have been upon losing my child. At least some of the terrain was familiar.

A few years ago, while going through a tumultuous time of re-grieving my parents and rethinking my relationship with them, I sought out Jewish tradition for comfort, guidance, and the gift of a day of rest. I began to attend Shabbat services, to pray for Noah, and to cultivate gratitude and compassion. That start at a spiritual practice and belonging to a supportive Jewish community give me a wellspring to draw from today when the pain is overwhelming. I'm grateful for that foundation, even as I still feel abandoned by God.

Passover: More than Four Questions—@ 13 months

Last year, Noah agreed to make his aunt's delicious macaroons for our Passover Seder. A week later, he was dead. Instead of ten people at our house for a ritual meal, we had 100 for a *shiva* memorial service. Instead of the four questions of the Seder, we have endless questions that will never be answered.

Why is this year so horrifically different from all other years?

Why did a plague of darkness descend on our son?

What do we tell the child who is too fearful and ashamed to speak his pain?

Why didn't the angel of death pass over our house?

Bryan and I couldn't face hosting Passover so soon after Noah's first death anniversary last year and were fortunately invited to a friend's house. We were able to enjoy the evening. But it's hard not to lose myself in the salt water and horseradish on the Passover table, symbols of bitter tears and slavery. It's easy to forget the boiled eggs, symbolizing hope and rebirth, and the sweet *haroset* (fruit-nut spread) that are also part of the ritual. We're meant to meld the symbols together in a traditional sandwich of *matzoh*, *haroset*, and horseradish. Noah used to join in the bravado at our Seder over who could tolerate the most horseradish.

Will this once-precious holiday always be tainted for our family?

As we remember Noah's love for Passover and other family gatherings, can we allow the sweet to outweigh the bitter?

In contemporary interpretations of Passover, Jews are encouraged to ponder our personal *mitzrayim* (Egypt, narrow place, oppression) and envision crossing over to freedom. Like our ancestors, we're invited to decide what to leave behind and what to take with us on the journey.

How long had Noah suffered in that narrow, constricted place in his mind?

How ready am I to leave behind self-blame for failing to save my child?

How can I carry with me the image of my son strong, healthy, and alive?

When will I be freed from the need to be a mourner with grief the center of my days?

Missing Atonement/At-one-ment—@ 19 months

The second Yom Kippur since Noah's death was intense but easier than last year. Our grief was more silent and contained, more numb than raw. I still cried during the Yizkor memorial service when the rabbi suggested we think of being in a room with our lost loved one walking toward us. I wept at the sung promise to pass on the tradition "from generation to generation," as we have one less stake now in that future. It was still jarring to move between the hole in our hearts and cheerful new year's greetings to family and friends.

Like last year, I refrained from life review and repentance. Having struggled with so much guilt, remorse, and anger around Noah's suicide over the past year, I held back from rehashing it or going deeper. Instead, I tried to focus my atonement on one moment: the last words I said to Noah on the last night of his life.

Noah had miraculously run a marathon the day before, despite debilitating depression. I told him how proud of him we were, what an accomplishment it was, and how it showed he could set a goal and meet it even in the hardest of times. Then I nudged him to set small goals for himself and start taking steps toward them, like finding a psychiatrist and getting a part-time job. I know now how insensitive this was. I saw his despair but I didn't grasp how he was too far gone to make those phone calls. I'm appalled that this was Noah's last impression of me— unless he registered the goodnight kiss that I blew him later. I'll never know if my pushing him that night with expectations he couldn't meet was a trigger for his suicide the next day or if he was acting on a prior plan he'd made—or both.

What I do know: Without atonement, there will be no at-one-ment with Noah's spirit.

Third Passover: *Dayenu*—@ 24 months

We're still in denial, not wanting to face preparations for another family holiday without Noah, especially one that came only a week after his death.

So when a friend brings up the word *Dayenu* for contemplation at our Jewish meditation group, it takes me a while to face it. *Dayenu* is a popular song during the Seder that recounts the miraculous events in the Exodus story and at the end of each line says *Dayenu—it would have been enough, it would have sufficed*. As in: *Had God brought us out of Egypt and not divided the sea for us, Dayenu*.

I knew that I couldn't say *Dayenu* for the years we had with Noah because 21 years are not nearly enough. My first impulse was to try to say *Dayenu* to Noah for all the things that didn't happen but could have had he lived:

Had you come home from college and taken a long break to rest and heal, Dayenu.

Had you taken a long break and decided not to go back to school, Dayenu.

Had you not gone back to school and drifted for a time without a focus, Dayenu.

Had you drifted for a time and kept us at a distance, Dayenu.

Had you kept us at a distance and tackled your demons on your own, Dayenu.

Had you vanquished your demons on your own and lived an ordinary life, Dayenu.

I wish Noah had known that it would have been enough had he simply lived; we and others would have loved him and helped him however we could. But would I truly have had compassion for his continuing struggles? Would I have accepted his choices, his limitations, the possibility of our continued estrangement? Before I'm engulfed by that sea, other verses come to mind to clear a path:

Had we had the loving support of family but not that of friends, Dayenu.

Had we had the loving support of friends but not that of our community, Dayenu.

Had we had the caring support of community but not the help of support groups, Dayenu.

Had we had the understanding of support groups but not that of therapy, Dayenu.

Had we had the insight of therapy but not the healing of nature, music, and yoga—Dayenu.

Had we had the healing of many things but not the health to restore our lives, Dayenu.

This litany, more in the spirit of *Dayenu*, could go on for many verses. We're deeply grateful for all that helps sustain us through grief.

Ayeka? Where Are You?—@ 30 months

In the new tradition of Jewish spirituality, Rabbi Jill Zimmerman (2015) invokes the transformative potential of God's call "*Ayeka*? (Where are you?)" in the Torah and the response "*Hineni* (I am here, I am present)." She teaches that when God calls "*Ayeka*?" to Adam and Eve in the garden, God is asking about their spiritual state. In the story of the burning bush, when Moses answers *Hineni*, he signals his readiness to hear God's voice. At any moment in our lives, Zimmerman suggests, we can challenge ourselves with the question of where we really are in our spiritual development, and we can strive to be fully present in responding *Hineni*. She likens this to waking up.

I've been asking myself *Ayeka?* all through this grief journey. My writing is testimony that I am here, surviving, and present to the grief in my heart. The more time that passes since losing Noah, the more confidently I can raise my voice to say *Hineni* rather than feeling small and despondent. As grief loosens its intensity, I have to remind myself to ask the question. When I take the time to check in with my inner state, I can collect myself, feel more deeply, and reconnect with that grieving, loving place. That gives me a bit of peace.

TO MY FELLOW SURVIVORS OF ANY
FAITH OR SPIRITUAL BENT:
Have you managed to stay connected to sources of spiritual sustenance? Do you or those around you stop to ask *Ayeka* (where are you)? Do you take time to check in with your grieving self as part of your spiritual practice?

Candle and Blessings Meditation
These meditation practices can be meaningful for people of all backgrounds.

Candle Meditation
In a quiet, darkened room, light a holiday or memorial candle. Sit comfortably facing it, breathing easily, allowing your body to relax. Gaze softly at the flame. It's OK if your mind wanders; just keep returning to the candle as your focus. If you wish, think of the light that your loved one brought to your life and the light you brought to them. Imagine all that light filling your soul and illuminating your way as you continue your grief journey. Sit with this peaceful moment as long as you like.

Blessings Mantra

This is to say inwardly as a focus during meditation, coordinated with your breath, with or without the Hebrew, in any order:

- May I (he/she) be blessed with *shalom* (peace).

- May I (he/she) be blessed with *simcha* (joy).

- May I (he/she) be blessed with *chesed* (lovingkindness).

- May I (he/she) be blessed with *rachamim* (compassion).

- May I (he/she) be blessed with *shlemut* (healing, wholeness).

Adapted from Jewish meditation practices

Chapter 9

WHAT IS LEFT
Remembering and Forgetting

Changing the relationship with the person who died from one of presence to one of memory and redirecting one's energy and initiative toward the future often takes longer—and involves more hard work—than most people are aware. We, as human beings, never resolve our grief, but instead become reconciled to it.

Alan Wolfelt (2009)

On Curating My Son's Legacy—@ 3 months

I took on this job without being asked. I became the curator of my son's legacy, his spokesperson to the world now that he can no longer speak for himself. This task has often consumed me in the past three months, giving me something to do to stay connected to Noah and channel my grief.

It started a day after his death when I copied a passage from Kay Jamison's (1999) book on suicide about how love for and from others is no match for the inner demons of mental illness, and showed it to everyone. People were grateful; we all needed to make sense of an inexplicable act. I would later come to regret this hasty grab for explanations and to question whether Jamison's account represented Noah's experience. But I was already framing his life and death for others.

A week later I was fielding dozens of e-mails from students and staff at Noah's college, who were planning a memorial service.

Would we allow the college to name the death as suicide to quell rumors and allow the community to deal with it honestly? (Yes, absolutely.) Did we want the Jewish mourner's prayer as part of the service? (Yes, we were reciting it daily, though it had no meaning for our son.) Was there a quote or poem for the program? (We could only think of the traditional Jewish saying, *May his memory be for a blessing*.) Students briefed me on plans for a slide show, a photo exhibit, a dumpling dinner; I thanked them over and over for being his friends. I felt the need to say something reassuring to everyone, given that Noah hadn't said goodbye to anyone. This was exhausting.

Then there were the long weeks of trying to reconstruct a fuller picture of Noah's history by talking with his friends and therapists and perusing his personal writings—private jottings never meant to be seen by others, much less prying parents. We had to represent our son's personality, relationships, and habits in the fractured way of parents who knew less and less about their child after he moved away from home. Did he hide a drug problem, like he hid his suicidal thoughts? As curator, I dutifully compiled Noah's psychological history in a six-page chart of life events, behavior, treatment, and excerpts from his writings so we could show it to professionals for a psychiatric autopsy. Like any curator, I had to know my subject and make choices of what to include and what to leave out. Will I regret these decisions later when I see things differently?

How Noah would have hated his mother speaking on his behalf and crafting a story of his struggle. He was 21 and desperate to be independent. It's not about how Noah would want to be remembered; we can never know that. He left no note, no instructions; he sought oblivion. Now it's about how we the living want or need to remember him.

So in choosing paper for his memorial scrapbook, I look first at the bold, geometric prints that Noah might have liked. Then I realize I'm the one who will be making this book and looking through it for years to come. I choose papers in the softer colors and subtler patterns that I find pleasing.

Memory Shift—@ 4 months

Memories of Noah are shifting, as if seen through a kaleidoscope.

At first, I was haunted by images of Noah dead and Noah suffering; all I could remember was recent time when he was severely depressed and not himself. Trying to piece together the puzzle of his state of mind kept me submerged in trauma. I couldn't face looking at pictures from happier times; they seemed distant and unreal, tainted by the specter of suicide.

Then I spent a few weeks sorting through photos and other people's memories while preparing a scrapbook for Noah's birthday. I paged through the book incessantly while assembling it, seeing the gradual accretion of a different story than the mental health history I had so painstakingly compiled. The scrapbook is a gathering in of interests, phases, people, and talents in Noah's life, a testimonial to its richness. There are separate pages for his model rocketry days and juggling performances, his college costume parties and his pizza-making days in France. There he is swimming or goofing around with cousins, partying or hiking with his best friends. "He lived more in 21 years than a lot of people do in 80," said a fellow survivor when she saw the scrapbook. To see this both pleases and dismays me.

How did Noah get from all that curiosity, energy, and zest for life—from being what a friend called a "Bunsen burner of joy"—to despair and the violent ending of life?

Maybe the memories will keep shifting, the sweet with the painful, until they settle into a balance we can accept.

Forgetting—@ 5 months

Forgetting

Our young dog, set free
on a beach for the first time,
stares up at us in disbelief,
then romps
along the scalloped foam,

dashes
full speed toward a dog
unshackled in the distance,
doubles back to galumph
over breakers and chase
rafts of pelicans,
hundreds of them,
floating, flying,
nose-diving to a prize
the dog cannot reach.

Our young son, gone
these five months,
would have raced him,
shouting,
into the surf.

For a few minutes
we forget.

Let's Talk of Epitaphs—@ 7 months

Let's talk of graves, of worms, and epitaphs;
Make dust our paper and with rainy eyes
Write sorrow on the bosom of the earth

Shakespeare, Richard II

Bryan and I have an appointment at the mortuary this week; it's time for us to talk of epitaphs. For months, I couldn't face writing Noah's dates or imagine words for his gravestone. These words will be written in stone, outlasting all of us. The epitaph that "writes sorrow on the bosom of the earth" and the placement of the stone over his grave will seal the permanence of Noah's untimely death.

Where to begin to sum up a life? A list of interests and hobbies seems trivial. Some possible one-liners:

Adventurer
Tender soul
He made things happen
Bunsen burner of joy
Full of life
So many gifts

I'm leaning toward *so many gifts*. So many gifts that Noah possessed, so many that he gave family and friends over the years. The gifts Noah had and shared in life are how I'd like to remember him and have others remember him.

We can never capture who he was and how he lived in a few lines. So we gravitate toward the simple and heartfelt:

Much loved
Much missed
Forever in our hearts

Will any of this feel right a year or 20 years from now? At a loss for words.

Listening to Sadness—@ 8 months

You learn a lot about people after they die. This is especially true after a suicide, which plunges the living into desperate rifling through the remains for any clue to the unraveling of a mind. When people share their memories, you seize upon each one in the hope that it will unearth another breadcrumb along the path.

So it was when I received the treasure of a compilation of memories from Noah's college friends. In most, I recognized the young man he'd been a year or two before his death—his humor, his many passions, being "always down for any adventure." But some spoke of a kindness I'd never seen in which Noah reached out to put people at ease, even sought them out in moments of sadness to listen to their troubles, as four friends described:

> *I had been sitting there under a tree crying for a while without anyone talking to me when Noah walked by. Even though he had no idea who I was, he sat with me, asked me what was wrong, and talked to me for a while before persuading me to come eat lunch with him and his friend.*

I would run into him with my head about to explode, and he'd listen and be generous with his time. He listened more genuinely than most people I know.

He had this ability to be so warm so fast and seemed not to allow you to feel strange or timid or anything when he was around. This quality is so rare and it's unreal that he's not here to be that person for so many of us anymore.

His impulse to give, to listen and to be there, unequivocally—this is a quality that never disappeared, even when he began to struggle more and more visibly.

As I read these accounts, I remembered that Noah met his girlfriend when he noticed her standing alone looking glum at a party. He was drawn to sadness in others, maybe because he recognized parts of himself that he rarely expressed. Not knowing how to voice his own depression, he wanted to see how others navigated it—or to offer them the listening and comfort that he craved. I'll never be able to mull it over with him as we did so many things in our years-long conversation. What I do know is that the people around him felt heard, understood, befriended. And that my son was a *mensch* for reaching out to them.

Pride is not easily come by after the destruction and hurt of a child's suicide. But I'm proud that Noah, as he was becoming the man he could have been, had the heart to listen to and lighten the sadness of others. Even if he ultimately couldn't let in others to help himself.

What is Left—@ 9 months

All the sweetness is gone. Those wide, all-seeing green eyes. That full, springy head of hair and loping gait. That vitality, curiosity, and marvelous conversation. The promise of Noah growing into his adult self while I grow old, bringing more life into mine.

What's left is the chill of the glass in picture frames when I try to kiss Noah's head. Brief jottings in his college notebooks, full of despair and poetry I never knew he had. A small box of mementos that he put together after cleaning out his closet a few months before his death. (He'd lingered over his things for hours that day in an uncharacteristic silence; was he already contemplating the end?)

They say that those we've lost live on in our hearts and memories. Maybe so with people who die a natural death after a long life. When someone dies by suicide, the pain, confusion, and bitterness can block the way to memories. "It's hard to remember tender things tenderly," as Karen Green (Silverman, 2013) wrote after losing her husband, the author David Foster Wallace, to suicide.

Or as the pop singer, essence, put it in "Shape of You," *Is sorrow all I have left of you?* (essence & Pease, 2009).

Letting Go, Holding On—@ 22 months

I'm one who holds on. I think friendships should last a lifetime. I never know when it's time to put something aside to clear the way for something else. I hold onto life and can't imagine doing otherwise.

Noah let go of everything. The instinct of self-preservation no longer had a hold on him. Letting go of life must have felt like his only way out of pain.

I cling to every memory I can muster, as to a lifesaver.

When Noah was eight, our extended family was on a small fishing boat in the Galapagos that sailed between islands at night. Noah was horribly seasick; he never went below and could only sleep outside on a bench on deck not far above the surface of the water. He was so skinny and light, I worried that he'd be tossed overboard. So I held onto him all night and told him to hold onto the railing. We held on together through the pitch and roar of the open ocean. Each morning, we emerged in the quiet bay of an island to walk among magical creatures.

How I wish I could have held my son through the storm that engulfed him 13 years later and been a beacon to safe harbor. I never dreamed there would be a morning without him in it.

As a child, Noah marveled at the iguanas, tortoises, and blue-footed boobies of the Galapagos. He loved swimming with the sea turtles and adored the round-eyed, whiskered fur seals, who reminded him of his dog back home. One night on deck, we saw a fur seal sitting regally atop the landing skiff that we towed behind us, hitching a ride. As we moved in for a photo, the seal dove over the edge and was gone.

I'd like to think that Noah's spirit is still tied to us, holding on for the ride.

Memorial Bracelet—@ 28 months

A good friend helped me design a memorial charm bracelet, which she had ready for me on day one of year three since Noah's death. I love looking down and seeing this circle of Noah's life around my wrist, a constant reminder that I can see, touch, and kiss. Strung along the bracelet are:

- a dog charm for Noah's great bond with our family dog and other pets

- iridescent blue glass for his love of the ocean, surfing, sailing, kayaking, and traveling overseas

- a croissant charm for his time in France, his passion for cooking and good food

- a peridot stone for his beautiful green eyes and keen eye for photography

- three silver balls for his years of juggling with his dad and brother

- a gold pearl for his beautiful mind and tender soul

- a heart charm for all the love he gave and received

- my birthstone (amethyst) for his place in my soul and mine in his.

I wear the bracelet every day. I like to finger it in the dark and guess which charm or stone I'm touching. I like to shake and turn it on my wrist to admire the many sides of Noah that it holds. Sometimes I align the bracelet so his green eye faces up; *see where I am now, in Seattle, with your cousins, on that trail where you backpacked. Here's something you once saw or would have liked to see.* I like bringing Noah with me everywhere and having something beautiful to look at that reminds me of him.

I take it off only to swim. It's OK because in the water, I'm in Noah's element. I can't put the bracelet back on myself so in a silent ritual, I approach my husband with it draped over my wrist, and he struggles to find and cinch the tiny clasp. Each time we go through these motions, we seal Noah's memory between us.

Only a few people have asked about the bracelet. When another mother admired it and I told her it was a memorial bracelet for Noah, she flushed and winced as if sorry she'd spoken. When Noah's teenage cousin noticed it and I told her what it was, she said, simply, "I love you."

When Remembering is One-Sided—@ 29 months

I will remember you; will you remember me?

> Sarah McLachlan, Seamus Egan, and Dave
> Merenda, "I Will Remember You" (1995)

I've been so preoccupied with how we'll remember Noah that until I chanced to hear that line from Sarah McLachlan's plaintive pop song again the other day, I'd forgotten about Noah remembering us, his family. The silence at the end of the question sent me into a long crying fit in the car.

Mutual remembering is the bargain we strike with those we love, even if we eventually break up or lose touch. They matter to us and we to them; we've shared experiences together; we're different for having known one another. This bond makes us wistful at life's passages, from the end of summer camp to graduations and weddings.

It's an unspoken understanding between generations that elders won't be forgotten; the young will tend our shrines. They'll carry us with them in some piece of their appearance and habits, how they see and talk and act in the world; maybe they'll pass on some stray bit of us to the next generation. The whole taken-for-granted enterprise of family—what we bequeath to the young and how they receive or change or resist it. Our little toehold on immortality.

Suicide nullifies the bargain. We'll continue to carry our lost ones with us, but their particular way of holding us in their heart comes to an abrupt halt. What should be a mutual exchange becomes woefully one-sided. It's yet another way we lose a part of ourselves with suicide loss.

It strikes each time with a heavier sense of finality; the piece of Bryan and me that became part of who our child was died with him. Our particular spark will never move through Noah and be reflected by him and re-imagined and passed on to others. We'll never be regarded and remembered and loved in quite that inimitable Noah-like way again. We have to learn to live with the silence in this one-sided relationship of remembering.

Remembering Noah @ 25—@ 36 months

We've finally taken a step toward making Noah's memory make a difference in the world. Bryan started the paperwork for the nonprofit Noah Langholz Remembrance Fund. It will support suicide awareness and prevention programs, as well as organizations, causes, and activities that brought Noah joy, like international student exchange and photography. We plan to give the suicide-related donations each year around his death anniversary and the life-affirming donations each year around his birthday.

We're also planning a gathering to mark Noah's 25th birthday where those who love and miss him, especially his young friends and cousins, can remember him together. I hope the power of our collective memory will be a balm and a bond (see Chapter 14, Opening My House).

TO MY FELLOW SURVIVORS:
How do memories of your loved one sit with you right now? What ways have you found to perpetuate their memory? How would you answer the three questions for grieving people posed by John Schneider (1994, pp. 66–67) that he says can help transform loss into renewal: "What is lost? What is left? What is possible?"

Walking Mindfully in Beauty

Give yourself the gift of a meditative walk in a beautiful spot in nature or a lovely garden, maybe a place that your loved one enjoyed or that you visited with them. You may want to bring a picture or memento of them with you. Be mindful as you enter this space; notice it and your appreciation of it. Slow down to feel each footfall, from the heel to the ball of one foot, then slowly shifting to the heel and ball of the other. Breathe deep, take in the beauty around you, and tune into an image or memory of your loved one as you walk.

For more structured mindful walking, try Comins' (2007) Meditative 25-25-50 Walking:

- Stand still in nature, aware of your breath, letting thoughts arise and fade away (one minute).

- With half your attention still on your breath, focus the rest of your attention on the soles of your feet connecting with the earth (one minute).

- With 25 percent of your focus now on your breath and 25 percent on your feet, focus the remaining 50 percent of your attention on the beauty of the space around you as you slowly begin walking.

- Continue the 25-25-50 slow walk as long as you like, returning to the breath when your thoughts wander. Be present, moving, in the moment.

Adapted from Comins (2007, pp. 60–61)

Chapter 10

SOOTHING OUR GRIEVING SELVES
Comfort and Healing

The work of healing is about being present to your pain and honoring yourself through a regular practice of self-care and compassion... Ask yourself: "What is the most empowering thing I can do for myself in building a sanctuary for this journey?"

Dianna Bonny (2015)

What I Pray For—@ 3 months

I never prayed until Noah was in crisis. Then I prayed constantly for him to find a way to healing and peace. I was so focused on Noah as the object of my prayers that I didn't know what to pray for after he was gone.

What I pray for now is the wisdom and strength for Bryan and me to be able to voice our grief, cherish our child's memory, support others and ourselves, and restore our lives.

And in Kundalini yoga classes, I chant the closing hymn about being guided onwards by one's pure inner light. Now, instead of directing those words at Noah, I think of his family and friends who are hurting, including myself.

Jacaranda Therapy—@ 4 months

When a therapist suggested that I find calming colors to call to mind when flooded with traumatic images, I immediately thought of the deep lavender of the jacaranda tree, like a technicolor hue from another planet. Lavender was the color of gifts I exchanged for years with a best friend. It's the color of the light I sometimes sense behind my eyes after an especially deep meditation. To mark the two-month point after Noah's death, I wanted to surround myself with that color.

So I took a walk among the jacarandas on the Caltech campus, going up to each one to sit under it and receive its rain of blossoms. On the grass, puddles of perfect purple petals. In the pond, a smudge of purple rippling the surface. As I wandered from tree to tree, I cried for myself, for my son, for what might have been, and for all the wonders Noah will never see. In that enchanted place, I felt briefly blessed.

Yesterday, I was having lunch with a friend—the mother of Noah's oldest friend, who keenly feels this loss as a fellow mom—and she pulled out a framed painting she had made of a magnificent jacaranda tree. "For you," she said. How did she know? Now I see jacaranda purple on my bedroom wall every morning before I get up, reminding me of the possibility of gratitude.

Reaching for Poetry—@ 5 months

I was learning to write poetry in the year or two before Noah died. The day he killed himself, I had copies of two poems ready to bring to a workshop that evening—one about mourning for my parents, one about my father's suicide. How strange that I was already writing in the key of grief. I never made it to the workshop that evening. Instead, my house filled with wailing.

Since Noah died, I've been afraid to read poetry. Too many poets are depressed and suicidal. Too many poems take the reader to the most painful places, sometimes without warning. I can't take the risk right now.

Since Noah died, I've only managed to write a few fragments, like this:

How different the world looked
three weeks ago—
heaps of jasmine spilling
over the fence,
spring fever scent wafting
over the neighborhood,
a child healing, we thought,
licking his wounds
in the womb of our den.

Now, the blossoms brown and brittle,
the child gone,
a family ripped apart—
one desperate moment
that changes everything.

And this:

Orchid buds opening
one by one
each day
turning to the sun.
Hopes and dreams collapsing
one by one
each hour
for our dead son.

I'm far from the "emotion recollected in tranquillity" that Wordsworth (1800) says gives rise to poetry. I cling to these bits of poetry in the hope that I can reclaim my voice and find solace in the outpouring.

One Incredible Thing—@ 6 months

Amidst the shock and grief of the first days after losing Noah to suicide, there was one incredible thing. A friend was in the airport when she heard the news. After crying and talking loudly on her cell phone trying to make sense of what had happened, she was approached by a teenage girl with blue hair, multiple piercings, and tattoos, who gave her this note penciled inside a heart (names have been changed):

> *Hello there. I know I'm just a stranger in the airport but I'm writing this to say hello... I'm Allie, 15, going to be 16 in July... I heard your story; indirectly you have given me the will and drive to live... I've suffered from depression a while and at times was suicidal. I recently lost my step-dad, I've never known my real father. I would frequently self-harm and thought no one would care if I was alive or not... Seeing others mourn in a situation that could have easily been my own made me realize how valuable my life REALLY is...so thank you... Sorry if this is strange but I wanted to say thanks. You're beautiful.—Allie*

When my friend brought me this message from Allie, it stopped my tears for a moment. It was the only gleam of hope in a desperate time. My friend read the note aloud to the gathering at our house after the funeral. I posted it on my blog for World Suicide Prevention Day, when people around the world light a candle in the window to bring attention to those who died by suicide, those left behind, and those at risk for suicide. We'll never know if Allie's change of heart was lasting, but we know that the suffering she heard in my friend's response to suicide gave her a glimpse of the devastation that follows for survivors. And that, in turn, reconnected her to life.

As survivors of suicide loss, we want to stop the hand of would-be suicides—if not in our own family, then in another one. To say, especially to the young, who lack the life experience to know that moods can be managed and that calm can follow the storm, "With time, with support—it gets better." To say, especially to men, "There's no shame in getting help." To say simply, like Jennifer Hecht (2013), "stay"—for the sake of the people you love and your future self. If we couldn't change the trajectory of our own loved one's life, maybe, at least, we can help give someone like Allie a chance.

New Arrivals—@ 7 months

Two mysterious bird shadows strutted behind the gate in the dark when I got home from work the other day. They didn't look like our chickens, which would have been safe in their coop at that hour. When I flipped on the light, they skittered away—two beautiful black and white speckled Wyandotte pullets, peeping in confusion. They'd apparently been abandoned in our backyard.

What serendipity, new life left on our doorstep! We made feeble efforts to find the owners, knowing we'd keep the birds. They made us laugh with their lopsided sprints across the grass, the first to arrive when any snacks appeared. They did everything as a pair, chortling to each other like an old married couple. We called them Tweedledum and Tweedledee, Dum and Dee for short.

We delighted in their innocence. They reminded us of when our hens were young, when our boy was still alive and we were innocent of grief. New life that knew nothing of suicide.

I felt the same when I was handed a five-month-old baby to hold recently. Our eyes locked, I started to sing and bounce him, and he melted into a smile. *You're new and pure; you weren't yet born when my baby died seven months ago.* I breathed in the sweetness of a fresh lease on life.

What Noah broke; what those of us left behind will need.

Comfort Food—@ 9 months

Bryan has been making a lot of apple cakes lately. It started with a bumper crop of Fujis on his parents' tree and a yen to recapture the Old World comfort of his grandmother's apple cake. He experimented till he found the taste and texture he wanted. The apples have a fermented tinge that melds with the richness of the dough and the char of roasted nuts. Wherever we go lately, like a survivors' potluck, we bring an apple cake. Everyone marvels over it, as if reminded of their own grandmothers.

Maybe Bryan has been channeling Noah's spirit by spending so much time in the kitchen. Noah loved to cook and to eat. At age eight, he practiced flipping crepe-like Norwegian pancakes.

He got serious with French bread and *tarte tatin* as a teenager, when smitten with all things French. I picture his tall frame hunched low over the kitchen counter, overlapping apple slices just so in the pan. He and his cousin devised elaborate pizzas, and he perfected the art with an Italian friend in France. He made pizza, omelets, dumplings, and pasta dishes for college friends. He was almost as good as his dad at making *latkes* (potato pancakes) for Chanukah.

When Noah was home the last three weeks of his life, I tried to make nice meals in the hopes of pleasing him. He seemed moved to be at Shabbat dinners on Friday nights with wine, challah bread, candles, and blessings; there was a glimmer of feeling on his face that we hadn't seen in months. Once, I convinced him to make falafel together, but I couldn't get him to try a new baguette recipe or do much of anything with me in those weeks. He was already too far gone—from me and from life's pleasures.

The day of his suicide, Noah made himself a toad-in-the-hole breakfast, cutting a hole in a slice of bread in the pan and breaking an egg into the hole to fry and flip. Bryan later said he couldn't see why someone who was planning to kill himself that day would bother.

I feel listless in the kitchen lately. I've botched some dishes I've been making for years. I don't have the patience for new recipes; everything's too complicated. Cooking reminds me of my beautiful boy and all that we couldn't share at the end of his life.

I reach out for comfort food to remind me of love.

Our Grieving Selves—@ 10 months

At a drop-in support group for suicide survivors, a young woman who recently lost her brother was distraught seeing how other survivors were still upset years after their loss. "Does it ever stop?" she cried.

"We're not always like this," a more experienced group member explained. "This is where we bring our grieving selves because we know we'll be heard and understood."

Our grieving selves—a whole new self for many survivors, who must shed one skin and grow into another. We're no longer who we were. We don't know how to present ourselves to others with this stricken face, heavy gait, or unpredictable weepiness. How to walk the mourner's path out in the world when everyone else still plies their regular route? We may need to hole up for a while as we get our bearings. Eventually, we learn where we can bring our grieving selves and when it's best to leave them at home.

Eventually, we find that we're more than our grieving selves. We may not always need to give voice to our grief once past the most intense early period. One of Bryan's co-workers came to the door the other day, face serious, arms out to give a silent hug to a mourning mother. I happened to be laughing about something as I came to the door before I saw his face; I gave him a brief hug like I would have if I'd seen him at the office holiday party. The moment was jarring for both of us. I'm grateful when people acknowledge my loss in the depth of their gaze and the strength of their hug or handshake, if not in words. But at that moment, I wasn't thinking of Noah or needing support. Ten months after his suicide, I'm not always grieving, and that both surprises and confuses me.

I'm not always crying and missing Noah and trying to make sense of what happened. But when I am and want to share it with others, I bring my grieving self to my blog. Having that outlet takes the pressure off needing to unburden myself in social situations. In the blog (as in this book), my grieving self is expected and embraced. Thank you to everyone who reads this for welcoming my grieving self.

Promise Letter—@ 14 months

I heard a mother tell survivors how she wished she'd been with her son the day he killed himself and how a friend told her, "You *were* with him." We survivors need that reminder of our abiding love.

If you're a survivor, you might try making a list of all the ways you showed your love for your lost one, both in happier times and when they were struggling. You could do it on their birthday or yours, or maybe on Mother's or Father's Day if you're a parent. Maybe you wish you could reach out to that person and pour out your love. If so, you could try writing them a "promise letter" or pledge, detailing your commitment to them and their memory, as suggested in Anne Brener's (2012) *Mourning and Mitzvah*.

Here's part of a promise letter I wrote to Noah about a year after his death:

Dear Noah,

I will never forget you and my love for you and your love for me. I will hold you living in my memory, alive to possibilities, as you were for nearly all your years in the most wonderful way. I will tune in to your spirit when doing the things you loved. In honor of you, I will strive to be more free, adventurous, and relaxed. I will always believe that you could have been happy and had a good life.

I will continue to reflect on your life and death and try to understand you with compassion. With time, I will forgive you, myself, God, and the universe. I will carry with me from this journey the lessons of opening the heart, showing love, and truly listening to others. I will try to give your brother all the care and attention he deserves, with a warm and rich family life and everything I can do to nurture his health and happiness. I will dance when I feel like dancing, cry when I feel like crying, and sometimes both at the same time. I will try to do the things and be with the people that give me strength, comfort, and even joy. I will try to be happy and have a good life, though it will never be the same.

I will cherish your tender soul. I will write your name on every beach. I will love you forever.

Pilgrimage: What I Bring with Me—@ 14 months

I was excited to go on a pilgrimage, taking the same trip to Paris and Berlin that Noah planned and had to cancel due to his troubles. I wanted to visit the French host family that he lived with as an exchange student. He and the family became close during the formative year he spent with them, and Bryan and I became friends with them, too, bonding over our love of Noah, hiking, and travel. At the memorial for Noah on their houseboat the previous year, they collected messages and drawings from his friends and wrappers from his favorite wine and chocolate and piled them onto a tiny wooden raft that floated away down the river to the sea; they sent us a video of the gathering. Finally, I would get to hug this family and mourn with them.

As with each new milepost along this path, I was full of trepidation. Would I make the French family miserable with my crying? Bryan didn't feel comfortable traveling far from home—how would I manage without him and our dog and my healing routines? How would Bryan cope with being alone for two weeks?

I got frantic thinking of all the things I needed to feel safe while away. Then I realized I had what I needed to take care of myself if I could just remember to take things slowly and mindfully. I could always close my eyes and breathe deep. I could meditate, write, sing, or pray anywhere. Knowing that refuge lies within lightened my baggage. And just in case, I had a packet prepared by a thoughtful friend with one item to sustain me for every day of the trip—a poem, a quote, a letter.

The trip was packed with more pleasures than expected. I enjoyed retracing Noah's steps to a chateau, a wine cave, and an opulent railway station restaurant in Paris, where he told me that the exquisite dinner took five hours. I met more of his French friends. I talked and cried with his host mother, comforted knowing that she, too, is still grieving and trying to understand. I felt Noah's presence most when alone on the family's houseboat, a converted river barge. I could almost see Noah bounding down the wide stairs from the deck and gorging himself on Nutella and baguette with his host brother, his 17-year-old energy reveling in a new life and language. It was touching to stay in Noah's former room, a tiny, wood-paneled wedge of a sailor's bunk with a porthole and a postcard he'd put on the wall of Caillebotte's magnificent painting, "The Floor Scrapers."

From Paris, I went to Berlin to visit an old friend, just as Noah had planned to do. He would have embraced the funky, bohemian vibe of that city and joined the throngs of young people partying along the canals.

With each plane departure, I thought of Noah's ultimate leave-taking and of the endings that have become so difficult. In those moments, I intensely missed Bryan, Ben, and our dog.

I came home to the same unbelievable, heart-sinking fact of Noah being gone forever. My husband's loving welcome blunted the harshness a bit.

Making this pilgrimage felt satisfying, like closing a chapter. What's the next milestone?

The Gift of Flowers—@ 23 months

One hold on hope I've often sought out through this nightmare has been flowers.

Noah died in early spring. The mental fog of the weeks after his death mingled with the jasmine perfume seeping from vines on the backyard fence. Walking to synagogue, I stopped on every block to breathe in the scent of peach and purple roses along the way; once there, I took breaks in the garden, my teary face safe inside a billowy rose. I picked sprigs of lavender wherever I walked and kept them drying in my pocket to sniff for moments of calm. With an old friend, I exchanged close-up photos of magnificent flowers, wild and cultivated; *wish I could text you the smell*, we wrote. With another old friend, I went in search of wisteria and lingered in its enveloping fragrance. Eventually, Bryan and I were able to visit a rose garden without being overcome by the gulf between its perfect beauty and our empty hearts.

The star jasmine and the dog were the last living things to bear witness to Noah's fateful walk from back door to garage. The dizzying scent gave him no pause; he was past noticing. I want to see and smell these flowers and think of the sweetness of my child's soul. Each spring, there's another chance to transform these reminders of death into harbingers of life.

Love Tokens—@ 27 months

Bryan and I are on a three-week road trip, the longest and furthest we've traveled together since Noah's death. Bryan has needed to stay close to home where routines, familiar faces, garden, and pets are a comfort. Thankfully, our dog Lobo is traveling with us.

As we walked or rather, tumbled, across a wild beach in Oregon in a ferocious wind, I was cheered by Lobo's leaping and frolicking. I wasn't gazing out to sea seeking a flicker of Noah's presence, like I often do at the ocean. I wasn't even looking for a souvenir in the sand to bring home for his grave, a reminder of another trip he might have taken. I was present in the moment rather than dwelling on what was or might have been.

I drew my usual heart in the wet sand for Noah at the far end of the beach. The wind was already starting to blur the letters of his name as I finished.

Turning back against the wind, pinpricks of sand stung my cheeks. Hunched over, feet dragging, I focused on the small square of blowing sand in front of me. Suddenly, heart-shaped stones appeared underfoot, gray, white, and black, infused with evening light. They were rough and jagged but definitely hearts. This windswept beach was full of love tokens and I hadn't noticed. Here, unbidden, were signs from Noah or the universe, imperfect and precious. The more I looked, the more I saw.

What other little miracles have I failed to notice on this journey?

In Praise of Support Groups—@ 31 months

Support groups are a crucial part of the grief journey for many survivors after suicide loss. I've been part of three different groups and visited others, with the number of survivors ranging from two to 35. I can't imagine having come this far without the love and understanding of these groups.

The most important support came from the first group I attended, starting three months after Noah took his life. It was a comfort just knowing there was a time and place every week to focus on my loss, voice my grief, and be with other survivors.

I didn't have to worry about whether the people around me could tolerate my pain, whether I felt safe, or whether I'd be able to function. All I had to do was bring my grieving self into the room.

When I was most lost and distraught, that group showed me a way forward. It was led by a therapist and a trained volunteer, both survivors who are well versed in grief, suicide, and suicide loss. They offered not only compassion but invaluable perspective and resources that helped me begin to make sense of what happened to my son and what was happening to me and my family. Through the facilitators, I saw, dimly, that healing was possible, though it felt remote at the time.

In listening to and affirming one another, group participants made an abnormal experience feel normal and shared. When I recounted an insensitive remark made by a relative, they were instantly appalled and protective of me. When someone talked about not being able to go back to the home where the suicide occurred, everyone nodded. We shared our dread of holidays, anniversaries, packing up our loved one's things, going back to work. We congratulated each other on every small step. For 90 minutes a week, we didn't feel so crazy or alone.

In that group and others, I've appreciated: bringing in pictures of our lost ones; doing relaxation exercises and meditation together; hearing inspirational readings to close each session; lighting a candle for our shared losses; hearing just the right words at just the right time; turning all our care and attention to a new member who couldn't stop crying; exchanging hugs with strangers who became friends.

I've struggled at times, too, with these groups. I didn't meet as many other mourning moms as I wished. I got impatient with people who monopolized group time and with facilitators who didn't stop them. In the early stages, it was disturbing to hear about some methods of suicide or types of mental illness, histories of suicide attempts and hospitalizations, severe abuse or family dysfunction. I was burdened enough with my own story and not always up to hearing another tragedy or someone else's bitterness and anger when it was out of sync with my feelings—

so I tuned out for a while. Fear of being overwhelmed with others' troubles, along with fear of exposing their own, keeps some people away from support groups. I'm glad I persisted. It takes all kinds of support to move through the pain of suicide loss, so why not get as much support as you can from as many sources as possible?

Joining a support group for me was another step in "coming out" as a survivor and chipping away at shame and stigma. At its best, it's a privilege to meet people from all walks of life who share your pain and share their stories in a safe space, led by skilled facilitators. These fellow travelers can become your teachers, comforters, cheerleaders, and friends.

With deep thanks to all the suicide loss survivors, facilitators, and organizations that make these support groups possible. If you're a survivor who hasn't yet tried a group, I hope you'll find your way to the support you need.

(To learn about support groups in your area, check the websites in the Recommended Resources section at the end of the book. Both experts and survivors suggest trying a group a few times to give it a fair chance and allow you to get used to it. Some groups do pre-screening so you can talk with someone first before attending; they may advise you and your spouse or partner to attend separate groups, like Bryan and I did, to feel free to talk about your individual experience. Groups meet weekly or monthly; some are led by trained volunteers, others by mental health professionals. Most groups are open and ongoing, while others are closed and time limited; some people attend for weeks or months, some for years. Your experience in a group will depend on the qualities of the facilitators and members, as well as your stage in the grief journey and your willingness to share, learn, and ally yourself with this "club no one wants to join.")

Where Do You Get Your Strength?—@ 32 months

There's entirely too much praise in our culture for being strong in the face of death—for being stoic and "getting on" with our lives rather than giving ourselves over to grief. One of Noah's friends marveled at my strength after the funeral, maybe because I asked how he was coping rather than collapsing in tears. But the apparent strength of mourners may be an illusion: Just because we seem calm and functional one moment doesn't mean we're not overcome the next. No one who's grieving should be expected to hide or deny intense feelings in order to spare others, care for others, or quickly resume their routine—though I know this is especially hard for survivors who must care for children or family members who are dependent on them.

So I was surprised when the facilitator of a support group, after hearing me talk about trying to resist shame and stigma around suicide, asked, "Where do you get your strength?" I felt embarrassed for being singled out and hastened to point out the resilience of other group members who'd grown up with very tough family situations. I mentioned protective factors in my life, like parents who loved and encouraged me and the genetic luck of being born without a predisposition for despair.

I also gave credit to becoming acquainted with grief as a young person in the mid-1970s when my mother was dying of ovarian cancer. We joined a support group for cancer patients and their families that was ahead of its time in promoting open, honest talk about death and dying; I came of age thinking that was the right thing to do. I used to scoff at my mother's oncologist, who persisted in clapping her on the back with a jovial greeting and the empty promise of a cure, even as toxic yellow fluids pooled in her abdomen and the bones began to surface in her face. The cancer support group helped beat back my fear of death as I took care of my mother in the last six months of her life and allowed her to die at home.

Losing my father to suicide six years later, while hurling me into the pit for a while, ultimately bolstered my life force (see Chapter 1, Déjà-Vu). When Noah died by suicide, I knew or thought I knew the lay of the land ahead. I also knew that this time, I needed to fully express my grief, ask for help, and support my family. In the intervening years, my approach to grief had been shaped by Anne Brener's (2012) guided journaling and appreciation of Jewish mourning rituals.

Where do you get your strength? It's an important question for us survivors, a little like asking where we find hope or healing. The answers are often similar yet the sources of our strength are more deep-rooted, intertwined with who we are and how we've lived. We draw on everything we've got to move through this loss.

Some sources of strength for me come from luck or circumstances outside myself. I'm fortunate to have had access to therapy and, more recently, to support groups for suicide loss survivors, which didn't exist at the time of my father's death and still don't exist in many places. I've been blessed by companions in grief with every loss, especially this one—dear friends and cousins who know how to be present with gentle love, listening, and care. They offer what psychologist Jeffreys (2011) calls "exquisite witness" to my way of grieving. Sharing the loss of a child with my spouse also makes finding my way less lonely and frightening. And feeling the support of my Jewish community and tradition at milestones on the grief journey has been a revelation.

I've found strength in writing, singing, and spiritual practices that I was already cultivating before Noah's death. I believe that I need to express, explore, and understand my grief, and I gain courage from sharing that journey through my blog, this book, public speaking, and private conversations. I find strength in giving strength and comfort to others who are in pain. Strength, I'm convinced, comes from being fully present to our loss and having the courage to open our hearts and embrace vulnerability.

We don't always have to be strong. And we don't always have to be healing when we hurt so badly. Strengths are not necessarily accomplishments, and grief is not a task to be done right. Still, it's helpful to pause, name the strengths and supports we do have, and be grateful.

TO MY FELLOW SURVIVORS:
Where do you get your strength? Where do you find comfort? What additional comforts can you create for yourself out of self-compassion?

Restorative Yoga: Self-Massage

Restorative yoga is a gentle practice for release and deep relaxation that anyone can do with the aid of a few pillows and blankets (no experience necessary). It's a series of long, slow poses done lying down, best experienced with a teacher's guidance in a yoga studio or with a video.

Here's a taste of a slow self-massage that is part of some restorative yoga sessions. You might want to first put on some soothing music and make sure the room temperature is comfortable. Lie down on a mat in a relaxed position with pillows tucked under your head and knees, or if you prefer, sit well supported in a chair. Close your eyes and take plenty of time for each step:

– Start by rubbing the top and back of your scalp with your fingertips in a circular motion, then continuing on to your forehead, temples, and cheeks. Cup each side of your face in your hands and gently move the jaw and throat in circles.

– Massage the back of your neck, then your shoulders, arms, and hands, taking your time to rub the length of each finger.

– Sitting up if you need to, use the heel of your hand as you move in a downward motion over the center and sides of your thighs. With your fingertips, gently rub around your kneecaps in a circle in both directions. Then massage your calves, shins, and feet (don't forget the toes).

– Return to a relaxed, supine position, covered with a blanket. Breathe in a full breath through your nose; sigh audibly as you exhale through your mouth. Repeat the inhale and sigh it out two more times. Rest.

Adapted from restorative yoga practices

Chapter 11

THE HARD STUFF
Guilt, Anger, Shame, and Forgiveness

Forgiveness is not an emotion that spontaneously bubbles forth, erasing all evil and wounds… Rather, forgiveness is a spiritual state. A way of being in the world, a discipline… Forgiveness is like a bridge you seem to cross, over and over again. With every crossing, you discover that there is more. More darkness. More to forgive. More to learn. More light than we thought possible, just waiting to be released.

Karyn Kedar (2007)

"You Did All You Could"—@ 3 months

People keep trying to reassure me that I did all I could for Noah without even knowing what I did or did not do. Of course, they're trying to make me feel better. The rabbi's eulogy at the funeral said if we must think about the what-ifs, to go there as little as possible. But especially in the first couple months and still sometimes now, I need to dwell there; I need to grieve the enormity of my sense of guilt and helplessness. I didn't do all I could to help my child and prevent this catastrophe.

My doctor suggested making a list of what I did and didn't do to try to help Noah. Here's a short version for the last weeks of his life:

What I Did:

- helped him leave a stressful situation at college and come home

- gave him a list of psychiatrists and urged him to call

- cooked for him; tried to interest him in cooking and doing simple things together

- gave him space, let him rest

- tried to talk with him about his feelings.

What I Failed to Do:

- ask him again if he was feeling suicidal

- recognize warning signs like social isolation

- recognize that he was incapable of calling doctors

- bring help to him if he wouldn't get help

- bring friends to him if he wouldn't call friends

- read about major depression and its dangers

- hang out with him just to be together

- every day, tell him I love him and it gets better.

What did I fail to do, model, or instill, years ago that left Noah so unprepared for this crisis? I can't face that list yet.

"You did the best you could with what you knew at the time," a therapist tells me over and over. I can accept that idea a little better than a blanket pass of "you did all you could." Maybe what I can learn to eventually accept is my limitations. None of us do all we can; there are always constraints. The limitations of what we know and understand about the person and about the mind. The limitations of our personality and our relationship with the person in crisis. The limitations of not wanting to provoke someone who's already fragile or hostile. The limitations of our imagination—living in denial, assuming the person will eventually follow the healing script we had for them. The inherent limitations of what any person can do for another. As my husband, Bryan, says of Noah, "It was so hard to know how to help him."

TO MY FELLOW SURVIVORS:
If you feel burdened with guilt, have you tried making a list of the good things you did for and with your lost one? Maybe it will feel like far too little, too late. But you can keep adding to the list as you reclaim your memories and your relationship.

On Sin and Forgiveness—@ 6 months

I'm thinking a lot about sin and repentance as Yom Kippur approaches. In Hebrew, the word for sin means "missing the mark"—a gentler, less alienating concept. Noah's abandonment of life and my failings toward him both feel so far off the mark that the gentler wording seems laughable.

The first step in repentance in Jewish tradition is to face and name our failings. I've been endlessly cataloging the things I failed to do in the last months of Noah's life. I've cried out these sins to Noah at his grave and elsewhere. The list gets longer as I learn more about Noah's suffering.

The next step is to seek forgiveness from the people we've wronged. I used to write notes to my kids for this purpose in the days before the holiday. They never responded, but Noah valued the notes enough to save a few in his small box of memorabilia; I'll have to take that as his answer. One of the hardest things about suicide loss, especially with a rebellious young person, is that we lose the chance for future reconciliation—the validation parents hope to get once the fog of adolescent anger lifts and adult children can look back more calmly on their upbringing. I'll never have the chance to work out old hurts with Noah over a lifetime of relationship.

The third step is to forgive those who have hurt us. I'm still too angry and wounded for that. I don't believe that suicide is a sin in the sense of a moral breach that must be punished;

to believe that is to perpetuate the stigma that still surrounds suicide today. Yet at the moment, suicide feels like a crime against humanity, a violent upending of the natural order. Like murder, the act is irreversible and there's no way to make amends.

Marjorie Antus (2013) writes eloquently on her blog of how long it's taken to understand her daughter's suicide: "Knowing has given rise to forgiveness that I think, after 17 years, is finally in place." So I may be forgiven for not being ready to forgive after only six months!

I take inspiration from Joan Chittister, a Benedictine nun quoted by Antus: "Only if we can care for another enough to try to understand what drove the behavior that hurt us so, can we put our own pain down long enough to forgive. Forgive is what we do when our love is as real as our pain." Noah and others who take their lives couldn't put down their pain long enough to see the impact of their action on others or the possibility of another way out. Will I, too, as a survivor continue to be blinded by pain?

Lament for a Lost Child—@ 15 months

About a month after his death, I lamented for Noah. I adapted the words of a Greek folksong and added a wail at the end of each verse, as in:

> *What can I send you, Noah, there in the underworld?*
> *I send you an apple, it rots, a quince, it withers. Ay-eeeee!*

I learned to lament from the old women in a Greek village where I lived for a year in my twenties, doing folklore research that included attending a lot of funerals. Women used to gather in a tight circle around the body at the wake or around the grave at the memorial and improvise laments. They called out to the dead and to fate, rocked back and forth, and wept openly in shared grief. Their piercing cries were unforgettable and set off tears for anyone within earshot. Those women dressed in black taught me to give voice to pain. Maybe that's why I'm inclined to express, rather than contain, my grief today—and grateful to have a channel for doing so.

I've been composing a lament for Noah over the past year and just added more verses, which I sing to the tune of another Greek folksong:

Lament for a Lost Child

The stream is rushing in the canyon
Wildflowers coming into bloom
You're not here to see this springtime
Because you had a sense of doom

Refrain: How I wish that I had told you
Every day and every night
That I loved you and would help you
And everything would be all right

Everyone is grieving for you
Do you know how much you're missed?
No more late night conversation
No more curly head to kiss

I could see the darkness falling
Like a veil across your face
If you'd only gone for treatment
Could despair have been erased?

How I wish that I had listened
To the fear behind your eyes—
All the pain inside your silence
I didn't fully realize.

I want to take back what I said to you
On the last night of your life
Words I only meant to help you
Must have cut you like a knife

I'll forever beg forgiveness
For what I said and what I did
If I'd known, I would have done otherwise
But you kept the worst things hid

Refrain: How I wish that I had told you
Every day and every night
That I loved you and would help you
And everything would be all right

Dredging Up Anger 1: Raging Sorrow—@ 16 months

"It's a good thing they closed the coffin or I would have socked him one," said Ben after Noah's funeral. I couldn't blame him for being angry at his brother. All this time, I've seen anger as a natural reaction but didn't let myself fully feel it. Anger at Noah, that is.

It's been easier to fume at other people and things. I hate suicide and people who romanticize it. I hate rope and knots and how simple it is to end a life. I hate the gruesome suicide of Noah's good friend at college that I believe triggered his decline. I'm mad at relatives who couldn't speak openly with us about his death. I'm furious at psychiatry for its inadequate understanding and treatment of mental illness and suicidality. Why did it take decades and more than 1500 suicides to finally approve protective barriers at the Golden Gate Bridge in 2014? Suicide survivors often commiserate about these frustrations, tiptoeing around the real source of our anger.

How can I be angry at someone who was in desperate pain and not thinking clearly? If he was living with a mental health condition, how can I blame him? How can I rage when he's dead and gone, and no fuming will make things right? Anger gets tamped down by these rational thoughts and the need for compassion. It melts almost instantly into tears of frustration and grief.

Why can't I own and express my anger? It's lodged deep inside, stuck in the muck of this loss. It blocks my way forward, especially toward forgiveness. I have to dredge it up.

I try reciting rage directly to Noah, spitting and cursing into the wind as I take a walk:

How COULD you? How DARE you throw your life away and hurt us all so much?

You STUPID boy. You did a horrible, senseless thing that can NEVER be undone.

You didn't give yourself a CHANCE.

You BETRAYED us. While we were trying to help, you were planning this.

I gave you everything I had as a mother and you give me THIS?

I can't BELIEVE you left without a goodbye or sign of love.

I'm FURIOUS you're gone forever and I have to learn to live with you gone.

The words feel awkward, detached from my body. I'm fluent in pain but how do I speak anger?

Dredging Up Anger 2: Let It Out—@ 16 months

There's no need to force the anger, I tell myself. *Just let it out when it surges.* But my anger at Noah is so stuck, it takes an act of will to bring it to the surface.

I close all the windows in the house. I hit a pillow while shouting and am quickly exhausted. I punch and jab the air to loud drum music. Nothing feels right. Finally, I bring out a pile of newspaper and begin ripping it to pieces. With each tear come tears as I think how Noah's suicide RIPPED out my heart, TORE off a limb, SPLIT apart our family and peace of mind— and how I wish I could have TORN the demons from his mind and RIPPED the date he died from the calendar. The action finally fits the feeling.

Anger after suicide goes beyond words. It's not pure, clean rage but raging sorrow/sorrowful rage that's part of complicated grief. It's hard to be mad at someone for dying, like in the traditional stages of grief for a natural death, when they are the cause of their own death. The anger gets tangled up in other feelings before it can even speak its name. I have to learn to sit with it and make room for the unruly tumble that comes crowding in. No wonder it's been an unproductive summer, full of procrastination, fatigue, and resistance.

I'll keep looking for ways to tap into anger. Maybe yelling into the woods, finger painting on big swaths of butcher paper, or tearing out pictures for a collage, as Sharon Strouse (2013, p. 120) recounts doing in *Artful Grief: A Diary of Healing*. "I allow the coulds, shoulds and would haves to explode out of my guts," she writes. "I honor my rage and give it all its due" (2013, p. 121) in creating a collage like the masterful "Code Red," visible on her website.

Calling all old magazines! And recipes for anger unleashed.

(It can take a long time for anger after suicide to dissipate. For more than 30 years, I was furious at my father for the hostile act of calling me home from overseas and then killing himself just before I was due to arrive. I'd delayed coming home by a day so I could attend my best friend's wedding in New York; I always thought my father was punishing me for putting that friendship first. Then, two years after Noah's death, an unbidden memory of my father's last days floated to the surface. Before calling me home to Maryland, he'd asked my uncle to come up from Florida to help him organize his finances. Suddenly, I saw that with this request to put his affairs in order, my father was signaling an ending. Rather than trying to spite me with the timing of his suicide, he may have been sparing me the sight of his decline and summoning both me and my uncle to his home to make sure we'd be there to deal with the aftermath, together. Would I have recovered that memory had I not been learning about warning signs of suicide after losing Noah? Each loss sadly informs the other.)

Diminished—@ 17 months

Diminished

Held off
too many days,
the banshee
crashes the gate,
slashing, burning,
prying my heart loose
again.

I shed my life,
all I have been and known,
and shrink
to a tiny animal,
blind and mewling—
a speck of a bug
before the looming universe.

This is how it feels sometimes. Not right now, but last week. Not for days anymore, but for hours. Without warning, the whole big mess of a grief wave drags me under again—what Therese Rando (1993) termed a STUG (subsequent or sudden temporary upsurge of grief).

As time passes, I'm overcome with the flat finality of the fact of Noah's death. With each new step or insight, I realize how much of my self has been shattered by his suicide. I thought I'd faced down much of the guilt and remorse for not being the mother my son needed as he grew into adulthood and became unmoored. I can accept now, better than before, that I was hampered in helping him not just by my own limitations but by his secretiveness and refusal to get help. I can see how we survivors burden ourselves with guilt and an inflated view of our role in a desperate bid for a sense of control over disaster. But when a wave rolls in and knocks me over, it doesn't take much to fall into the pit.

Last week, Bryan was a steadying hand. He knew just what I meant about feeling small. We're neither of us who we were 17 months ago. We're bereft and diminished with everything about us and our world called into question. To move forward and reconstruct that world takes everything I've ever known and more.

Embracing Self-Pity—@ 17 months

Self-pity is taboo in our culture, tinged with shame like suicide. No one has patience with a "pity party." We're supposed to be strong in the face of grief. We're not supposed to feel sorry for ourselves or to want others to feel sorry for us. But with suicide loss, we can feel small rather than strong, less than instead of more than. We need sympathy and empathy from others, not just in the early months but later as bitterness sets in.

Maybe self-pity is part of the process. We survivors are the living victims of suicide. The lost one's pain is passed on to us, along with shock, remorse, abandonment.

As if there isn't enough guilt, I feel bad when I'm crying for myself rather than for Noah. A mother should feel her child's pain and howl at missing that child, and I do. Then sometimes, I tumble into the victim pit and feel cursed. I'm reminded of other losses—my father's suicide, and my mother's death from cancer when I was 19. Why doesn't anyone want to be in a family with me? Self-pity engulfs me and leaves me feeling small, helpless, and exposed. *Sometimes I feel like a motherless (and fatherless) child*—and a one-child-less mother.

I can't summon any strength or spiritual connection in those moments. I retreat and wallow. Maybe we survivors need those moments away from the stress of striving to reclaim our lives.

"A victim is a person who feels less than whole," writes Karyn Kedar (2007, p. 43). She urges us to "keep moving away from hurt, keep moving toward wholeness" (p. 22). She sees anger as an antidote to victimhood, a necessary stop en route to forgiveness:

> Well-placed anger is a healing agent. It tells you that what happened is wrong. Really wrong. It reminds you that you did

not deserve the offense… Anger can transform a victim into a person who believes he or she deserves goodness, wholeness and love. (p. 43)

That conviction of deservingness seems remote when I remember I'm doubly cursed by suicide.

My anger toward Noah gets spent in short bursts and quickly morphs into tears of self-pity. I need to give full vent to anger, yes. But I also need to feel whatever I'm feeling without judgment. *All emotions are welcome here*, says a sign at the Children's Memorial Garden where we have a stone for Noah.

TO MY FELLOW SURVIVORS:
It's OK to feel sorry for yourself. You've been grievously hurt. Sit with that as long as you need to.

Shaming and Naming—@ 28 months

I'm ashamed of how easily I can be sucked into the shame and stigma around suicide.

At my group adult bat mitzvah a few months ago, I decided not to include the part of my speech about suicide grief because I didn't want to dampen the celebratory mood of other families. As a result, I felt invisible during the ceremony compared to classmates who shared highly personal stories. A year earlier, when I read the bat mitzvah class a reflection on how Noah's suicide made me feel far from God, one person commented, "too much information." I felt shocked and shamed in spite of sympathetic hugs from other classmates. Is it any wonder I was wary of sharing my experience in public on our big day?

At family gatherings, I still self-censor and hold back from talking about Noah when he comes to mind for fear of bringing sadness, silence, and contamination into the room. Is this a surprise when most relatives avoid mentioning him?

On my blog, it took months for me to use Noah's full name rather than N. When I made the change it was a relief, restoring his personhood and our connection. I still kept my full name out of postings for fear that students or colleagues would search for my name online, see the blog, and judge me; I didn't want them to know this fact about me, especially if they didn't know me well. The blog still lists Mourning Mom as author. I had to check with my husband and son about using their names or Noah's last name in this book, lest it somehow harm them or taint our family name.

The most moving moment at gatherings of suicide loss survivors for me is always the closing ceremony when we light candles and stand in a circle, each speaking our lost one's name and their relation to us. Some people, like me, have more than one name to say. It's in those moments that I publicly own my experience as surviving both a father's and a son's suicide rather than focusing exclusively on Noah. We survivors stand up and speak the names of our lost ones with sadness, love, and pride. These names that are spoken less and less as time moves on. These lives that we'll never forget. In that setting, we stand together against shame and stigma.

I was amazed last year to see thousands of young people at the Alive and Running Run/Walk for suicide prevention in Los Angeles, noisily lining up for T-shirts and water bottles like at any fundraising race. Afterwards, I thought of changing out of my T-shirt when I went to a nearby café. But the cafés were full of people in T-shirts promoting the cause or the name of the person whose memory they were honoring. The S-word was outed on a sunny Sunday morning while other people enjoyed their brunch or cappuccino, and there was no shame. This gives me courage.

TO MY FELLOW SURVIVORS:
Do you ever feel that there's no place for you to express and work through the hard stuff? In addition to therapy and mind-body practices, try meeting other survivors, whether at support groups, online, or in private. Speak your pain; they can hear what you have to say.

Earth Energy Cleansing Flow

I learned a version of this Qi Gong-inspired practice on a retreat in the redwoods after a big cry. It's a good way to release the sludge in your soul that can build up after suicide loss. Ideally, try it in a quiet place outside where you can stand barefoot on the ground.

- Stand comfortably with legs hip-width apart, arms hanging, head and spine straight. Breathe naturally with your eyes closed or cast gently down. Feel your feet sinking into the earth and the earth holding them.

- On a deep inhale, visualize the powerful healing energy of the earth bubbling up through the sole of your left foot and coursing through your left leg and the whole left side of your body and arm, including your heart, filling you with love and light.

- On a long exhale, imagine releasing all your toxic emotions down through the right side of your body and arm, down your right leg and into your foot, allowing all the negative energy to drain away through your right sole down into the earth, cleansing you.

- Continue the cycle, slowly drawing in the earth's energy on the left side with the inhale, then letting it wash out impurities on the right with the exhale as it flows back into the earth.

Adapted from Milton (2006) and Rabbi Mike Comins

Chapter 12

PSYCHACHE
Facing Mental States
and Mental Illness

*The key, the black heart of suicide, is an acute ache in the mind,
in the psyche, it is called psychache. In this view, suicide is not a
disease of the brain; but rather it is a perturbation in the mind, an
introspective storm of dissatisfaction with the status quo.*

Edwin Shneidman (2008)

"It's a Tragedy. There's Nothing Anyone Could Have Done"—@ 4 months

"It's a tragedy," said a senior therapist at our HMO (health maintenance organization), shaking her head, when she heard about Noah's suicide. "This is the age when mental illness appears, especially in young men. There's nothing anyone could have done."

I'm outraged at this attitude. Are we to accept as inevitable that thousands of young people will take their lives every year? What's the point of mental health treatment and suicide prevention programs? The tragedy is not just that young people end their lives. The tragedy is that researchers' and clinicians' understanding of suicide is so limited, services and treatments so inadequate to the task.

I have much to learn about suicide and mental illness. But I have to believe that there are many points along the way to suicide when someone—or many people—could have done something. After all, in hindsight, we see warning signs and turning points. There are too many opportunities missed for intervention, too many chances of falling through the cracks when the stakes are so high.

Maybe it can't be helped that given their desperate push for independence, suicidal young people will often hide the extent of their problems, refuse treatment, and resist the authority of doctors or parents. But it must be helped when laws persist in treating 18-year-olds as adults who can take sole charge of their mental health without any parental involvement—this in spite of evidence of the brain's immaturity until after age 25 and the typical onset of mental illness coinciding with the years in which families lose all say in young people's treatment. And it must be helped when some clinicians believe there's nothing they can do to stop the scourge of youth suicide.

(I've since learned that many mental health professionals have had little to no training in how to recognize or treat suicidal patients. And of course, even well-trained clinicians and well-run hospitals lose patients to suicide. When patients die by suicide, clinicians are often beset with distress, guilt, and PTSD-type symptoms [Gutin, McGann, and Jordan, 2011]. The lessons they take with them from this experience can, hopefully, enlighten their colleagues and help more people in crisis.)

"Manning Up" to Problems—@ 5 months

While waiting in the airport to bring Noah home for a medical leave from college, I told him that we'd find therapy and medication that could help him. "I tried all that and it didn't work," he insisted. "I have to man up to my problems."

"What kind of bullshit is that?" I raged. I'd never heard such a thing from my sensitive son, raised by a feminist mom and a gentle dad. "Real men know when they need help," I said, but Noah only shook his head. I was too busy arguing with his words to hear the sense of an ending beneath them.

After Noah's death as I tried to fathom his descent into a black hole, I began to see possible roots of this "manning up." Older men he admired who urged others to "be a man" when they cried or despaired. College buddies who thought they were "bulletproof" after a friend's suicide. A cousin he adored who was "his own man," living alone in the woods and working with his hands. Macho movies Noah watched and screenplay scenes he wrote in his final months featuring tough guys so extreme, they seemed like caricatures.

Why should my son be immune to media messages about what it means to be a man? The more vulnerable he became, the more he believed he had to hang tough. Like so many young men, Noah didn't know what to do with sadness—where to put it, how to voice or channel it, how to ask for help when he needed it most.

I was horrified to learn that there's a whole class of young men in Japan who go into hibernation for years with depression, shutting themselves up in their parents' homes with video games. There are hundreds of thousands of these *hikikomori*, and they're considered at high risk for suicide. A Buddhist monk is trying to lure them back to life with support services and activities (MacFarquhar, 2013).

Maybe we have a parallel phenomenon in the US whose potential danger goes unrecognized. It's just boys being boys, retreating into the man cave and venerating tough digital guys. Noah didn't play many video games, but he got lost in that cave, groping for a way to man up and out. How can we shine a light on this cave and open the way to other paths toward manhood?

Fear, Shame, and Ignorance: What We Don't Know *Can* Hurt Us—@ 6 months

I finally read Iris Bolton's (1983) classic suicide loss memoir, *My Son...My Son...: A Guide to Healing After Death, Loss, or Suicide.* (Even the title makes me cry.) After losing her son, Bolton became a suicidologist and a founder of the suicide survivor support movement. She doesn't insist that suicide is caused by mental illness, like so many websites and booklets simplistically do today. Rather, she says it's complicated with many contributing factors, or what we now call "multi-determined."

This rings true. Because while the literature claims that more than 90 percent of suicides can be traced to mental illness, it also notes that the vast majority of people with mental illness don't take their lives. So there must be more to the story.

Lately, I'm convinced that in addition to the effects of insufficiently treated mental health conditions, Noah died from fear, shame, and ignorance. Fear of failure at college and of making his way in the adult world. Fear of another debilitating anxiety attack. Fear that he was losing his mind and that—much like my father—he would lose control of his life if he submitted to doctors, medication, and hospitals. Shame at the prospect of having a serious mental health condition and needing medication. Shame that he was unable to "man up" to his problems and that others ("everybody at college") knew something was wrong with him.

The ignorance belongs to all of us. To Noah about how to manage depression and anxiety and ride the ups and downs of young adulthood. To us his family about major depression, the severity of Noah's despair, warning signs for suicide, and how to talk to a suicidal person. To his friends who, like him, believed they could handle crisis on their own without involving adults. To professionals in three cities who only saw one small part of the elephant that was consuming Noah and didn't consider him a suicide risk. To the fields of psychology, psychiatry, and public health that still know too little about suicide and how to prevent it.

My own ignorance arose from fear of what I might learn. Why else would I start looking up "bipolar disorder" and "psychosis" online, only to stop after 20 minutes when it became too scary and confusing? I assumed too much and saw my son through the cloud of those assumptions. I assumed that I knew enough about mental health from my years of therapy, introspection, and probing conversations with friends. I assumed that, like my younger self, Noah could experience depression and still function in the world with his life force intact. I assumed that, like me, being exposed to suicide loss as a young person would make him stronger and more determined to live a good life.

I didn't understand that major depression can be a terminal disease or that losing a loved one to suicide can elevate one's own risk for suicidal thoughts and acts. I didn't know the importance of listening to a suicidal person's thoughts rather than immediately challenging them. And the most profound and troubling ignorance for a parent: I didn't know about my grown child's inner feelings and psychiatric history—the many things he didn't tell us that we only began to learn about after his death.

"You can only know what you know at the time," my therapist repeats like a mantra. You can't read your child's mind and we are none of us all-knowing. But what we don't know *can* hurt us, even destroy us.

(The more I read about suicide, the more complex the explanations become. Pioneering suicidologist Edwin Shneidman [2008], for example, believed that the root cause of suicide is "psychache," or unbearable psychological pain. He considered suicide multidimensional, with not only biological and psychological but sociological, epidemiological, and philosophical factors. Whether psychache ultimately leads to suicide, he wrote, depends in part on the person's pain threshold, coping skills, and support system [Leenaars, 2010]. When these various factors and conditions come together, there can be a "perfect storm" that leads to suicide [Jordan & Baugher, 2016]. This makes more sense to me than the mental illness explanation alone when I think of my child or my father. So, too, does Andrew Solomon's [2014] vision of suicide as a "crime of loneliness." Meanwhile, descriptions of impulsive suicides suggest that for some, easy access to lethal means at an especially desperate moment is all it takes, apart from any psychiatric history [Anderson, 2008].)

Coping Skills—@ 8 months

One of Noah's therapists was shocked at his suicide and dismissive of a tentative diagnosis of bipolar or schizoaffective disorder from the psychiatric autopsy. He said Noah had "poor coping skills" and lacked the patience to make a plan to fight his depression and anxiety.

I agree that Noah had a choice in how he dealt with his demons, at least in the early stages. I fault myself as a parent for not imparting the coping skills and emotional intelligence he needed to be resilient. He became overwhelmed with the enormity of forging his path in life at a time when he was also dealing with suicide grief from the death of his friend at college.

Another view of coping skills comes from the extraordinary suicide note of an 18-year-old girl, included in the book, *Dear Mallory*, by her mother, Lisa Richards (2012). Even when Mallory had good days, she wrote in her suicide note, "the pain I feel takes over every time. I've used coping skills—but I must be missing something because life shouldn't just be something to cope with" (p. 5).

True words, spoken with the youthful idealism and absolutism that Noah shared. Those with more life experience and perspective know we have to learn to cope with the hard parts in order to enjoy the gratifying ones. Yet unless we know how it feels when the hard parts become unrelenting pain over months or years, we can't appreciate how sensitive young people like Mallory and Noah may have tried to cope as long as they could.

After suicide, our loved ones no longer need to cope while we survivors must muster every coping skill we have just to get through the day.

Of Birds and Men—@ 10 months

We lost another beautiful hen from our backyard flock this week, with too many reminders of the fragility of life and our helplessness in the face of it. I couldn't help thinking of Noah.

Lulu got stuck in a narrow spot between fences, where a neighbor's dog attacked her wing. She set up an unearthly squawking that sent me running. Just as I tried to call Bryan the day of Noah's suicide, there I was calling him again. Just as my neighbor helped me after I found Noah, here he was again, valiantly cutting a hole in the fence to pull the hen out. When I put Lulu in a tall box, she immediately flew up and out into the garden. *Maybe she's OK*, I thought. That day, with Noah's skin still warm, *please let him live, please.*

A bird-lover friend told me that birds hide their ailments and act normal as long as possible so as not to attract predators; by the time they show their frailty, it's often too late. Bird owners must be vigilant to notice the slightest change from routine that might signal a problem.

Did Noah hide his problems as long as he could? Did he run around and try to mimic his old ways as a funny, fun-loving guy so as to distract attention from his suffering? Did we see signs of mental disturbance followed by near normal behavior and think he'd be OK? We didn't know how grievously he was broken till it was too late to reach him.

At the vet's office, we had to put Lulu down. Last year, we lost another hen to disease after nursing her inside for two weeks, two months before Noah's suicide. There's no comparison, none. But sometimes I think that those days nursing the ailing hen were a harbinger of what was to come when Noah arrived home from college for the last three weeks of his life. Our son, tall and strong but inside, weak as a sick bird. We thought we were being vigilant. It was so hard to know how to help him.

After the neighbor pulled Lulu out of her tight spot in the fence, he handed me a pale green egg, the first Lulu had laid in months. What gifts do our loved ones leave behind that are still too buried in sorrow for us to notice?

Valuing Life—@ 18 months

My son, Ben, fiddles with the map on his cell phone while driving on the freeway. "Please stop," I beg him, my voice rising. "I value your life." How many times I said that to my kids growing up! I said it to Noah about surfing, motorcycling, coming home late after partying. The more I said it, the more he tuned it out.

How I wish he'd taken it to heart.

How I wish he could hear it now.

How I never dreamed I'd have to learn how to value my child's life and my own after he destroyed one and devastated another.

After a suicide, we try to reconstruct the best parts of a life from the pieces on the floor and share them in memorials. We take on the valuing of a life that the lost one has abandoned. We look for meaning and connection, as best we can, where those who left us seemingly found none.

I hate it when people from wealthier countries (or neighborhoods) claim that people from other countries (or neighborhoods) "don't value life the way we do." We may condemn or be horrified by certain actions. But we can't assume to know how others feel about the value of life if we haven't walked in their shoes.

Noah should have valued his life enough to give himself a chance at a future and a healed mind. Maybe he valued life so much that he couldn't imagine continuing to live in the pain and shame that engulfed him.

Living with Your Mind—@ 19 months

"You have to live with your mind your whole life," a teacher told the novelist Marilynne Robinson as a teenager. "You build your own mind, so make it into something you want to live with" (Mason, 2014).

Bryan and I never said anything like this to Noah, but he knew that we relished the life of the mind. From about the age of 12, Noah set about building a beautiful mind—curious and passionate but also drawn to extremes and easily influenced by others. I felt lucky that Noah shared his thoughts with me well into his teen years. He absorbed ideas effortlessly as a teenager, like the positive psychology of Jon Haidt's *The Happiness Hypothesis*, detailing the very strategies he could have used later to combat his own depression. "Never have I met someone more naturally energetic, willing to engage (even if this just meant playing devil's advocate), and do everything in his power to keep things interesting," his college roommate wrote. "If you're going to argue for argument's sake, take the most ridiculous side you can possibly think of," wrote another college friend in her speech, "Lessons from Noah," at his college memorial. Also on the list: "Never be afraid to call something bullshit" and "Conversations are very important."

The mind Noah built began to fail him at some point and he panicked. Did he have cognitive problems first, like reading difficulties, which spiked his shame and anxiety? Or did untreated depression, anxiety, and PTSD compromise his thinking? Did Noah come to feel he could no longer live with a mind that had been ambushed by forces beyond his control and that without his mind, he was no longer himself? His mind was clear enough to know there was a problem but too tormented to conceive of healing and change.

How we would have loved to see where Noah's mind would have taken him as it grew past his 21 years. How, now, to understand and honor that mind?

Inside Out: Animating Sadness—@ 28 months

Bryan and I have been looking for fun, escapist movies in the past two years. We routinely reject movies that deal with death or troubled people; I can't even enjoy cozy British mystery shows if they dwell too much on dead bodies. Who knew that a Disney-Pixar movie full of the usual cleverness and whimsy would remind me of Noah's struggles and bring on tears?

Inside Out (Lasseter, Docter & Del Carmen, 2015) animates the inner workings of the mind of 11-year-old Riley, with Joy in charge of the other emotions (Sadness, Anger, Fear, and Disgust) in a storehouse of colorful balls (memories). Riley is a happy kid until her family moves to another city. Suddenly, Sadness tinges Riley's sunny memories with blue and she sinks into an uncharacteristic funk. As memories are tainted, entire "islands" of experience—family, friendship, sports—lose their color and motion and collapse. Joy and Sadness go on a quest to retrieve Riley's lost "core memories" and revive the islands that make her who she is. Ultimately, it is the power of Sadness that brings Riley home after she runs away, prompts her to speak her heart, and allows the family to reunite around supporting her in her troubles.

I couldn't help thinking of Noah's despair when I saw everything in Riley's world being touched by Sadness, over and over. "I can't help it!" Sadness says, and indeed, Noah's depression seemed to have a life of its own. Each time I saw Noah in 2012, his face was more drained of humor and color, his talk more constrained. By the time our family took a weekend trip to wine country in August, Noah sat slumped and silent at the dinner table. Like Riley, he became a shadow of his former animated self. It was sadness that made him notice others who were lonely or unhappy and reach out to them. Yet he was ashamed of his own sadness and convinced he just had to "man up" to his problems.

As Sadness took over in the movie, Riley's mind reeled out of control. Memories started to dim, as they may have for Noah. When Riley's islands of experience started to crumble in the movie, so did I. Watching each island self-destruct on screen was like watching the dissolution of Noah's mind, piece by piece. The longer Noah suffered from depression and anxiety, the more he lost his wit, confidence, pleasures, and connections. I felt helpless as I watched the windows of his mind go dark, though I always believed they could be lit again.

When Riley finally confesses her sadness to her parents, she says she was afraid to talk about it because she knew they wanted her to be happy. Did everyone's high expectations drive Noah to silence and shame as sadness became more overwhelming? Noah once told me that no one really knew him. Did I argue too much with his despair rather than really listen so I could give him hope?

Psychologists who consulted on *Inside Out* wrote that it's about "what people gain when guided by feelings of sadness"

(Keltner and Ekman, 2015). "Its central insight: Embrace sadness, let it unfold, engage patiently with…emotional struggles" in order to build new identities.

If only we could rewrite the script for our lost ones. If only we survivors understood what is to be gained from embracing the Sadness they left behind.

Denying and Accepting Mental Illness—@ 30 months

I'm haunted by lines from psychiatrist Kay Jamison's (1999) *Night Falls Fast: Understanding Suicide*, in which she describes her suicidal feelings as a person living with bipolar disorder. The prospect of suicide, she writes, was

> the end of what I could bear,…the final outcome of a bad disease. No amount of love from or for other people—and there was a lot—could help… Nothing alive and warm could make its way through my carapace. I knew my life to be a shambles, and I believed—incontestably—that my family, friends, and patients would be better off without me. There wasn't much of me left anymore, anyway. (p. 291)

I seized on this explanation just days after the suicide: Noah was cut off, on another planet, literally beside himself. I made a copy of the passage for my in-laws and had a friend read it aloud at the shiva gathering a day after the funeral. "It's the chemicals in the brain," someone told me there; "mental illness is a terrible thing." Dazed, I figured she was right. But later I was mortified that I'd been so quick to imply that Noah had bipolar disorder when the evidence for it was murky. I didn't fully accept that depression and anxiety could be mental disorders, given how those conditions occur along a spectrum including the "worried well." I didn't know that anxiety attacks can be scary, disabling, near-death experiences, and that Noah had been experiencing those often. And I didn't realize that Noah could have been living with PTSD with delayed onset in response to his friend's suicide in 2010, which put him at greater risk for suicide.

While Noah was declining before our eyes, I went in and out of thinking he might just (just!) be struggling with typical young adult angst. He had a penchant for drama, despite his laid-back California persona. When he was little, he was so used to being healthy that on the few occasions when he had a tickle in his throat, he'd come running to me crying, "Mommy, I can't swallow!" Years later, could he have had an outsized reaction to navigating a challenging college and finding a direction in school and in life? He hadn't faced much hardship or competition till that point and may have panicked at unfamiliar feelings of insecurity.

The link between mental health conditions and suicide can feel threatening, especially to families like ours with little experience of the mental health system or the label "mentally ill." Noah didn't have a history of mental illness, substance abuse, or self-harm, as far as we knew. Our family never had to deal with the diagnosis of a severe, chronic condition and a series of treatments for Noah, much less contend with hospitals or police. We didn't see Noah as living with mental illness partly due to fear and ignorance, but also because he hid his anxiety attacks and suicidal feelings, didn't allow us to consult his doctors, and seemed to have only sporadic bouts of odd behavior. It's hard to accept the label of mental illness now when Noah's not here to speak for himself or be properly diagnosed.

The closest I came to seeing Noah as mentally ill was during a psychotic or possibly mixed states episode that lasted about ten days, during winter break from college three months before his suicide. At first, it was bits of odd behavior: a shopping spree to buy used cameras; a sudden plunge into glum silence after a day skiing, ignoring the visiting cousins he adored; abruptly leaving a movie in the middle without explanation. One morning, he got up early rather than sleeping in and paced and smoked while spouting his philosophy of art and obsessing about his grandfather dying (he was fine) or a girl he knew being raped (she was fine). Over the next few days, he asked for my advice about trivial things, made numerous quick phone calls, and cried in short bursts. When college friends came to visit from out of town for New Year's Eve, he was silent at dinner and went to bed early instead of celebrating with them. He was uneasy about seeing a friend who'd made a suicide attempt a few months earlier but decided to go anyway; he called me later, desperate to get home immediately. (Another anxiety attack?) That day, after trying and failing to take a nap, he began sobbing and let me hold and comfort him for a few minutes for the first time in a long time (and, as it turned out, the last time ever). A few of Noah's old friends, to their immense credit, called to tell me they were worried about him.

Through all this, Bryan and I hid the car keys and pleaded with Noah to go to a psychiatrist, but he refused. I asked Noah if he was suicidal and he scoffed that he would never do such a thing: "You're the one with the problem, Mom," he said. "Maybe you should go to the psychiatrist." We spoke with therapists and psychiatrists we knew about the possibility of psychotic depression, Bipolar II, adverse reactions to drugs. I called our HMO repeatedly to see what our options were for having Noah seen and was repeatedly told there were none since he was over 18. When his symptoms subsided, we thought they might have been triggered by stress, drugs, or untreated depression. Since he refused to be evaluated during or after the episode, we had (and still have) no clear information or diagnosis.

I'm ashamed that I didn't take seriously the few hints Noah may have dropped about mental illness. "I have so many voices in my head, I don't even know which one is mine," he told me in his last weeks. I should have asked what he meant and really listened. Instead, I assured him we all have many voices in our heads and can spend years seeking our own authentic voice. I saw what he said through the lens of "normal" experience. But Noah may have meant, literally, voices, including those telling him to kill himself.

Jamison (1999) says acute psychological stress is one of the three causes of suicide, along with genetic predisposition and a major psychiatric illness. The college years bring on acute stress for some students; in one study, about a third report feeling so depressed in the past year that they couldn't function (NAMI & Jed Foundation, 2016). Depression is common in college, along with excessive risk-taking, anxiety, changes in mood or sleep patterns, and use of drugs or alcohol—five of the ten warning signs for mental illness. So of course, "it can be difficult to know whether what you are experiencing is an early sign of an emerging mental health condition or part of adjusting to college," according to a guide for students (NAMI & Jed Foundation, 2016, p. 8).

Is it possible to dread another anxiety attack so much that you work yourself up into life-threatening spirals of fear? To obsess and anguish so much that you literally drive yourself crazy, without being chronically mentally ill? To contemplate and complete suicide because you can't bear the pain, yet not have an underlying mental disorder? I'm still learning about and pondering these questions.

I've been in big denial about Noah and mental illness. With time, I'm moving toward acceptance that he likely struggled with an elusive, untreated mental health condition, on top of his own suicide grief from a friend's death and difficulties finding his way in college. When I feel angry now about his suicide, it's less anger at Noah for being stubborn about treatment and letting himself deteriorate. I'm more often mad now at circumstances, at mental illness itself, and at fate for giving my child a losing number in the genetic lottery. I'm learning more about families that live with mental illness and realizing that we probably did, too. Except that unlike families who were experienced with psychiatric diagnoses and treatment for their child, we faced the puzzle of our son's erratic behavior without understanding the gaps in the picture or knowing the rules of the game.

"His illness moved faster than his acceptance of it," family members said at the funeral of another promising young man who took his life (Jamison, 1999, p. 67). How can I fault Noah for rejecting the bleak future that he assumed was inevitable if he saw a psychiatrist about agitation and delusions during or after his psychotic break? Most of Noah's life had been about growth and accumulation of friends, experiences, skills. Maybe he couldn't face the possibility of life as a person with a mental health condition, which he assumed would be all about loss, limitations, and stigma for himself and those who loved him. (He would have scoffed at the sanitized term, "mental health condition," and said, "They think I'm crazy.") Noah's illness moved faster than his or my acceptance of it.

The "100% Preventable" Myth—@ 31 months

We get such mixed messages. "If they're determined to kill themselves, they'll find a way," my doctor claims. Yet the suicide prevention field implies, by its name, that tragedy can be averted. Some groups even claim that suicide is "100% preventable," a misleading message that has been picked up by the news media and many websites.

Ronnie Walker (2014), founder of Alliance of Hope for Suicide Loss Survivors, documents the stigmatizing effect of the "100% preventable" message on suicide loss survivors. The claims reinforce our sense that we did not do enough, even if our loved ones gave no sign of suicidal despair or intentions, even if we strove mightily for years to help them. Walker suggests we look on 100 percent preventability or zero suicide as a "possibility" for the future but recognize that we have a long way to go as a society to meet that goal. Organizations like the American Foundation for Suicide Prevention have set the still ambitious goal of a 20 percent reduction in the suicide rate by 2025.

From what I've learned, many suicides are preventable—up to a point. Suicidal people are often convinced that they're worthless and a burden to others, who would be better off without them (Joiner, 2005). Their thinking becomes constricted, believing that there is no way out and that things will always be this way. They may no longer be able to feel or to care about others. At that point, they can experience the tunnel vision or voices in their head that lead only to thoughts of suicide, putting them in a kind of "suicide trance" (Heckler, n.d.). That seemed to happen with Noah as he moved through the last few weeks of his life in a daze, barely able to converse, much less call a psychiatrist. He may have had the sense of entrapment common to people in crisis, feeling that he could no longer keep up his lifestyle and the self-image he projected and seeing no alternative. The challenge for family and friends and for the field of suicide prevention is early detection and intervention: recognizing when distressed people may be moving toward that point, convincing them to get help, and continuing to show them our love and concern.

Many survivors live with the tension between believing that the suicide could have been prevented and having felt powerless to help the suffering person. Some of us get involved in suicide awareness and prevention efforts, as I have, in the hope of saving even one life, yet at the same time wonder if such efforts would have made a difference for our own family. I doubt that Noah would have ever called a crisis line, attended a mental health lecture, or sought out a peer counselor at his college. Likewise, I assume my father was too spooked by the threat of hospitalization to call the community crisis line where he used to work as a volunteer or to confide in a friend who was a psychiatric nurse.

Suicide may not be 100 percent preventable, but we can and must do more as a society: destigmatize mental illness, help-seeking, and suicide. Fund prevention research and action, as well as accessible, effective mental health services and peer support programs. Ensure that mental health and health professionals are well trained in suicide risk identification and treatment. Do innovative outreach to at-risk populations, like the interactive Man Therapy videos of the Carson J. Spencer Foundation or the "it gets better" campaign to combat bullying and depression among LGBTQ youth. Educate young people in coping skills and mental health literacy, and make such training standard not only at schools and colleges but at workplaces and health organizations. Put barriers on bridges and other suicide magnets, for God's sake! Let's support steps like these 100 percent.

Stay: An Inoculation Against Suicide—@ 33 months

I inoculated my kids against the usual preventable diseases. I exposed them to lots of enriching activities and discussions to engage them in life. I never knew I needed to inoculate Noah against the temptation to suicide.

I just discovered a vaccine that I wish he and other young people had absorbed as part of their education: Jennifer Michael Hecht's (2013) *Stay: A History of Suicide and the Arguments Against It*. Hecht writes that we owe it to our community and to our future selves to hold on through difficult times—that staying alive is a courageous, heroic act:

> None of us can truly know what we mean to other people, and none of us can know what our future self will experience. History and philosophy ask us to remember these mysteries, to look around at friends, family, humanity, at the surprises life brings—the endless possibilities that living offers—and to persevere. There is love and insight to live for, bright moments to cherish, and even the possibility of happiness, and the chance of helping someone else through his or her own troubles... The first step is to consider the arguments and evidence and choose to stay. After that, anything may happen. First, choose to stay. (p. 234)

Hecht's message is precious with or without the impressive history of Western philosophy and religious thought that supports it in the book. She contends that modern secular thought made a "wrong turn" in insisting on, even glorifying, the individual right to suicide in the face of despair; Camus's views, for example, have been misunderstood. Hecht lost two close friends to suicide and developed her thesis to provide "conceptual barriers to suicide" akin to protective fences or walls on bridges. I believe these concepts should be introduced when young people's beliefs are forming to counteract cultural messages that suicide is a right and a romantic, viable exit option, especially for artists and other sensitive souls.

For most of his adolescence, Noah and I had long talks about ideas; they mattered to him, just as Hecht insists they matter to people's views of suicide. It chagrins me to no end that Noah and I were too estranged in the year or two before his death to talk about anything important. What if one of his teachers or fellow students had floated Hecht's argument at a moment when he was open enough to hear it? What if Hecht's book was required reading for college freshmen? There's a chance that the idea of his "future self" might have made an impression on Noah and been stored away as a hedge against a desperate act. Especially since Hecht (2010) acknowledges the "monster" of depression and the suffering it brings: "Sobbing and useless is a million times better than dead," she asserts as she urges distressed people to hold on. "Thank you for choosing sobbing and useless over dead."

As for me, I so miss not having the chance to know and love my child's future self.

(Another inoculation that I came to wish I'd given Noah in his teens was "the talk" about depression, which should be as common as "the talk" about sex. I should have told him that depression runs in the family, that it's biologically based and nothing to be ashamed of, and that with the genetic lottery, it could affect him or his offspring. I should have told him the symptoms to watch for, how to ask for help, and the treatments that are available when he could still hear what I had to say. But I didn't have the knowledge at the time, the sense of urgency about the message, or the tools I needed, like the helpful booklet, *Starting the Conversation: College and Your Mental Health*, produced by NAMI and the Jed Foundation [2016]. We need to make such information required reading for teens and their families, handed out in schools, recreation centers, religious institutions, and doctors' offices.)

The Marathon Paradox—@ 37 months

All this time, friends and doctors have marveled that Noah was able to run the Los Angeles Marathon in the midst of major depression, only two days before his suicide. How could someone who was suffering like Noah was summon the energy to run the 26.2 miles that even healthy people can find daunting? One psychiatrist, the friend of a friend, was so intrigued that he offered us a free consult for an informal psychiatric autopsy.

Bryan wasn't surprised that Noah accomplished the feat and did so without even training. "He was young and strong," Bryan said. "He'd done marathons before and he knew he could do it again." Noah had run/walked several marathons and half-marathons with his dad, grandfather, and great-uncle in what became a family tradition. He knew the drill of getting up early, squeezing his way to the front of the crowd near the starting line, and pushing himself past the tough 21-mile marker to the finish.

When saying goodbye to his few remaining friends at college in February, 2013, Noah told them he was going home to run the Los Angeles Marathon in March; he mentioned no other plans. As the event neared and he showed no sign of training, I asked if he still planned to run and he said yes. The day of the event, I offered to pick him up anywhere along the race route if he needed to stop. A few hours later, he texted, "Just passed 19. Going to the finish." He looked no more exhausted at the end of the race than he had in previous years. He wanted to go straight home, though, rather than go out to celebrate.

When I told Noah's marathon story to a fellow survivor and marathon runner, she nodded knowingly. "Running is the easiest thing to do when you're depressed," she said, assuming you have some basic fitness. "The goal and the course have already been laid out for you. All you have to do is put one foot in front of the other to get there and accomplish something." Running marathons began as a refuge from depression and grief for this friend after her father's suicide and later became a joyous entrée to group camaraderie and world travel.

So maybe the pursuit of a tangible goal and the momentum of previous races carried Noah through the miles. Did he consider ditching it all and disappearing into the city? Did he think: *My race is almost run. At least my family can be proud of me for this*? Did he already have a plan for suicide and the marathon roused him to action? The last photos we have of Noah are the ones I took when we came home after the race. At first, he barely smiled in his exhaustion but then he rallied, grinning down at the dog with the old brilliant smile that we hadn't seen in months. Then he looked straight into the camera and smiled again, a bit more stiffly and sadly. A few weeks after his death, I realized that photo was his goodbye to his family.

The Inquisition: Why Didn't I See?—@ 42 months

It's not only the whys and what-ifs of the reasons behind Noah's suicide that will never be fully answered. It's the persistent whys behind my own ignorance and inaction while he was still alive.

I'm an educated, well-read, introspective person who had years of psychotherapy. Why was I blind to the dangers of major depression, anxiety disorder, and PTSD in my child? Why was I dismissive of the genetic and biological components of mental disorders?

I can only say I was too upset and confused to think clearly, especially in the last few months of Noah's life. I was on high alert, paralyzed by fear and worry. I grew up with my father's dim view of medication and the belief that nurture (and therapy) mattered more than nature for the psyche. Even as evidence grew in recent decades for the impact of brain biochemistry and medications on mental health, I didn't revisit that bias and inform myself.

I'm a college professor and professional researcher. Why didn't I research everything I could about my child's symptoms—at least those I knew about—and possible treatments? Why didn't I look up the warning signs for suicide?

During Noah's psychotic episode, Bryan and I spoke with friends and relatives in the mental health field and got a mix of explanations and advice. I did some online searches but couldn't make the information I found fit Noah's behavior. "Stop going online!" Bryan shouted when we argued over how alarmed we should be. "It's full of misinformation; it'll only make you more upset." I blame myself for not persisting with the research, though I'll never know if anything I missed reading or hearing might have made a difference.

I knew about groups like National Alliance for Mental Illness (NAMI); I even knew people who were active in a local chapter. Why didn't I seek out NAMI support groups and informational meetings to help me with Noah's mental state?

That's easy: I thought NAMI was only for the families of people with schizophrenia and other chronic, severe conditions. I bought into the stereotype and stigma that mental illness is someone else's problem. Noah's psychotic episode was a scary window into the unknown. But his delusions and agitation subsided, he went back to college, and we thought maybe his frightening behavior had been a drug-induced aberration.

Hope against hope: That's what many of us do when a dear one is in crisis or in the early stages of the onset of a mental disorder. We still see the person within the framework of who they've always been, even if something's different and concerning. We explain away anything odd, hoping it will pass. We can't instantly flip the frame we've always used to make sense of the person in our minds, to admit that they've changed and may have little control over that change. As Jill Bialosky (2011) wrote after her sister's suicide:

> The suicide leaves a map of her fate long before she dies. Love blinds us to this. We go to sleep. We wake. We pray. We hope. We wait for the leaves to turn a different color. But we rarely expect the worst. Or imagine that when crossing the street and a bus passes by our beloved feels herself wanting to be sucked under. We don't want to think of those we love being in life-threatening pain. (p. 197)

Then there's the question that cuts to the core, put to me recently in a writer's workshop: "Didn't you think that if major depression killed your father, it could also kill your son? Did you draw a line between those two things?" I didn't, at least not consciously. You can't see the pattern when you're enmeshed within it and scared. My father's suicide was a lifetime and 3000 miles away; there were few reminders of him or his death in my married life and few people still alive who knew him. I knew little of my father's psychiatric history and never saw him seriously depressed. I never related the struggles of a lonely, habit-bound, middle-aged man dealing with early retirement to the struggles of a popular, adventurous young man having an identity crisis. Except, of course, for that moment of panic in the plane flying east to bring Noah home from college, when I flashed on flying home to disaster with my father and promptly put it out of my mind.

What if I'd grieved the loss of my father differently and had the benefit of survivor support groups in the 1980s? What if I'd fully informed myself about depression and suicide back then, followed the huge developments in the field since that time, and faced the prospect of mental illness in the family? What if all this led to talks with my kids about mental health, resilience, and help-seeking? If I'd done even some of those things, at least my response to Noah's decline might have been different.

Enough with the inquisition! I wish I could purge the whys and what-ifs about myself that bring such shame and remorse. All I can do now is to learn more about mental health conditions and suicide and help others to see, to know, and to act.

What Matters—@ 42 months

In the end—and this is all about the end—it doesn't matter whether or not Noah was living with a mental illness or which diagnosis is correct. It doesn't matter exactly what toxic mix of genetics, biochemistry, life history, or circumstances led him to kill himself. What matters is that he was in unbearable pain, he couldn't fix it, and he didn't trust others to help him fix it.

With those stark facts in mind, how can I blame Noah for his suicide? By the end, he was no longer himself. The Noah whose action so grievously hurt me can't be held accountable, nor can he ever make things right again. He's beyond the realm of accepting fault or seeking forgiveness.

What matters is that I cherish the memory of my beautiful son with boundless love and compassion. And that I tell my story to help ease the way for other struggling young people and their families.

TO MY FELLOW SURVIVORS:
The suicide loss community believes that postvention (support for survivors after suicide) is part of suicide prevention for

survivors and others. How can you bring your story and what you've learned as a survivor to those who are struggling or to their families, friends, and communities? How can we promote a massive vaccination campaign to inoculate more suffering people with the urgent message to "get help" and "stay" before it's too late?

Self-Percussion to Expel Stress

Sometimes the pain is overwhelming and we just want it out. Whatever our sources of stress as we try to heal after suicide, we hold a lot of tension in our knees. Try these steps to expel stress:

– Sit on the floor with your legs stretched straight in front of you or sit upright in a chair with your feet solidly on the floor. Do each step below for at least a couple minutes.

– Begin by slowly massaging your knees with a gentle circular motion of your fingers, first one way, then the other.

– With palms flat, beat your open hands alternately (first one side, then the other) over each leg just above the knee; do this quickly and vigorously (it should be loud!).

– Next, make fists with your thumb inside your other fingers. Beat your fists alternately up and down the length of your outer thighs, quickly and vigorously.

– With hands still in fists, do the same alternate beating motion up and down your inner thighs.

– End by massaging your thighs in slow deep strokes from the top of the thighs to the knees. Sit with eyes closed and feel the effects of the exercise.

Adapted from yoga practices and EMDR preparation exercises

Chapter 13

PHASES AND STAGES
The Passing of Time

It seems to me that even though grief experiences can be very different, everyone goes through at least 3 similar phases. I call these phases 'living in the fog,' 'living with the questions,' and 'living into new skin'... John Schneider, Ph.D., says that at first a person who is grieving can only see what is lost, then they begin to see what is left and finally they are able to see what is possible.

Janie Cook (2010)

What's Shifted, What's the Same?—@ 3 months

I re-read my journal from the first two months. A lot of the rage, remorse, and tortured speculation still cycles through my mind. I can also see how much has already shifted, from the immobility of complete devastation to the first tentative steps toward resuming my life.

Some things I couldn't do at all in those first several weeks that I can do more easily now:

- set aside nightmare images from the scene of death

- wake up without always thinking of Noah

- walk more than a block or two

- listen to music or read novels (some)

- see young people enjoy themselves

- have conversations without always mentioning the suicide

- read or listen to the news (some)

- cook for my family

- sit through a yoga class or religious service without crying

- look at photos (some).

I'm no longer in such a state of raw shock; I'll be better able to cope with time. But I don't want to feel pressure to speed recovery or reassure people that I'm better.

Among the things I still can't do:

- forget the horror of March 19

- get through the day without crying

- put away the what-ifs, should-haves, could-haves

- decide what to put on Noah's gravestone

- erase him from my phone or address book

- plan for the future

- accept that my child is gone.

Drifting Away—@ 4 months

It's 16 weeks now since Noah left us and life is somehow moving on. Normal activities are starting to feel a bit more normal, though we're still stunned and fragile.

I hear that mothers can experience the death of a child as a mutilation of their own body, as physical as pregnancy and birth. Even mothers who didn't bear their children are intimately physically bound to them. Expectant parents count off the weeks during pregnancy or adoption and infancy with anticipation, marking each new beginning. Mourning parents count down the weeks, dreading each new ending that takes us further away from our child.

Slowly, as we take in the reality of Noah's passing, Bryan and I are starting to let go. The memorial services, the clearing out of Noah's room, the finishing of his scrapbook each close a chapter. His springy hair, wide green eyes, loping gait—all are beginning to recede. The living child and the horrifically dead child are both drifting away. Time is starting to turn Noah's life, with all its beauty and messiness and suffering, into memory.

New parents, with each week, feel the miraculous growth of love and family; mourning parents, on a reverse journey that was never meant to be, feel the pain of each small goodbye, each realization that our child is really gone. Saying goodbye to the joys that might have been, had our child given himself a chance to heal and grow into adulthood. Goodbye to our beloved boy, goodbye to what we knew as family. Ahead is unknown territory, how we'll reconstruct our lives.

Dread of Dates—@ 5 months

Dates loom large lately.

There's the date when everything changed: March 19, 2013. The dates of severe panic attacks we didn't know about before Noah's death. The dates in the past year that we had no idea would be his last birthday or Chanukah. The dates marked in his calendar for trips never taken and deadlines for college papers never written, along with all the blank dates left in 2013.

I see a random date on an e-mail, photo, or work document from before March 19 and my heart clenches: That was then, when we were still innocent. We had no inkling of the disaster that would upend our lives. I yearn to go back to the most ordinary day from that time and hold onto it—to climb the tower, like in *Back to the Future*, and turn back the clock. I would freeze it in August, 2010, when Noah was looking forward to his sophomore year of college, before his life was derailed by a friend's suicide.

I cringe to write the dates 1991–2013. The narrow span of Noah's life leaves me speechless. Those dates on his gravestone will define him for the world. I can't bear to write them in his scrapbook because to do so would mean The End.

The weeks and months unravel since his death. The shock of the first two months, the chilling reality of the next two months, the struggle to balance bouts of despair with slowly starting to reclaim our lives. My calendar is already filling with obligations—days without time for grief work, memories slipping through my fingers. The prospect of the first anniversary of Noah's death next March, the unveiling of his gravestone, and all the painful anniversaries to come.

Time moving forward without Noah in it.

Compartmentalizing—@ 8 months

When someone asks how I am these days, I usually say OK, as if worried about reassuring them. A more accurate answer would be, "I'm compartmentalizing" or "I'm coping."

As hard as the first raw period of shock and grief is, the later stage of re-entering "normal" life and switching back and forth between mourning and functioning can be even more draining and discouraging (Dyregrov *et al.*, 2012). Bereavement trails us like a scent; we rarely feel fully present in the world we used to inhabit. This can be true after any major loss but especially after the devastation of suicide.

The energy it takes to tamp down the grief and compartmentalize in order to function and accomplish other things in the world! I toggle back and forth between the work files on my computer and the ones named Noah's Life and Death, Grief, or Suicide Info. It's easier to switch files than to switch gears between my griefworld and the "normal" world. The more I compartmentalize, the more numb I feel; grief recedes further into the distance.

They say grief is a rollercoaster with its unpredictable twists and plunges. But for me instead of ups and downs, it's more like plateauing *numbs* and downs. I'm glad for the moments of forgetting and grant myself grief holidays sometimes. But I feel most alive, most close to Noah and my love for him, when I give way to grief. When I hold back because I have to function in the world, the grief only presses more insistently later. Tears are a welcome, cleansing release that take me far out to sea. When each bout subsides, I grope my way back to land and stumble around for a day or two till I find my balance.

Fighting Numbness—@ 13 months

Numbness can be worse than grief, as Anne Morrow Lindbergh (1993 [1973]) and others have noted. I know that numbness is a natural reaction, protection from being overwhelmed. But when I'm numb for more than a day or so, I feel disembodied and out of touch with missing Noah. Anguish builds up and needs release; I feel so much better after I can cry again.

When I speak to groups of college students about suicide awareness, I tell the story of Noah's suicide without choking up. That must seem unreal, even callous, to my audience. I do this to stay focused on the message of not letting fear, shame, and ignorance prevent people in crisis from getting help or those who love them from reaching out. The next time I speak in public, I'll explain that I still cry plenty when alone; my deadpan delivery is part of the numb spells and compartmentalization that are also part of suicide grief.

To fight the numbness, I recently went back to the mind-body therapy, EMDR (Eye Movement Desensitization Reprocessing) (see Chapter 2, Trauma in the Body). I need help reconnecting with my grieving self and confronting anger and guilt. Each session is cathartic and surfaces new insights, the polar opposite of numbness. Still, with each session draining me for a day or two, I find myself wondering how much more of this intensity I want or need!

There are other, gentler ways to stay in touch with our grieving selves, as Janie Cook (2014) reminds us in her blog, although "we often resist paying that painful attention... When we take the time to stop, take a deep breath and collect ourselves in the present moment, we give our spirits time to catch up with our bodies." I give myself moments for spiritual catch-up when I stop to write, meditate, pray, or do yoga—and when I allow myself to crawl back in bed some days.

Wrestling with Time—@ 24 months

From the day of Noah's suicide almost two years ago, time was frozen in shock. Bryan and I remained suspended in disbelief for months. One ruined day or night merged into the next. Calendars with future dates, pointless except for memorials; prior dates, precious because Noah was still alive. We hated time, so desperately did we want to wrench it back. The ordinary time we took for granted we'd always have with our son was snatched away. How could we possibly move forward?

Time hangs like a hammer, sings essence in her moving grief song, "Shape of You." *Will it ever, ever be/Time for time to pass?*

Grief is supposed to get easier with time and mostly, it has. I feel less buffeted and bereft, with shorter crying spells. I can usually function in the world and find things to enjoy, no longer seeing everything through the lens of loss. I can even choose when and how I mourn rather than feeling overwhelmed. Last night, for instance, I thought of looking through a box of Noah's memorabilia, but I was tired and watched TV instead.

Before the first anniversary last year, we were re-living the trauma of Noah's decline, his last days at home, finding him dead. If Bryan had taken a final hike with Noah on March 5, he was thinking of that on March 5. If my last conversation with Noah was a Monday, I was ruing that day as the clock ticked down. This second year, we're less tied to haunting dates.

The other day when I saw a sign with instructions for CPR, I flashed on the neighbor who rushed to help when I found Noah hanging in the garage. Things could have been worse without the neighbor, I tell Bryan. We go over each moment in the fateful day's events, weeping at the kitchen table. "I wish you didn't have to be the one to find him," Bryan says, twice. "It's nobody's fault," I say. Except Noah's. And not his fault either if he was ill.

I want to compile all our photos and videos of Noah in one place to be sure they're safe and accessible. "What's the rush?" says Bryan. He isn't ready to archive his son. He wants to keep stumbling on stray photos and e-mails. There's a lifetime ahead of us to mourn and remember. If we do it all now, what will be left?

But if we wait, what will be left? Already, so much has happened without Noah. The young people in his world have moved on with their lives while he stays forever 21. His untimely death hijacked time, held back the waters for a long, ghastly moment like some parting of the sea. But eventually, the waters closed around his absence, filling it with the onward rush of life. We want to remember, to hold on and feel the presence of our lost ones, but the traces of them dwindle, crowded out by the pressing needs of the present. At least, that's how it's been for me as the years go by after each loss. With time, there's less room for the dead in our lives, less occasion to think of them and cry for them. Maybe that's natural. I just can't bear to think it will happen with my child.

More seasoned survivors say that with time, we find a new place for the person in our hearts. Right now it feels like yet another layer of loss: The same time that heals also carries us further away from our loved one and our love.

A Shrinking To-Do List—@ 33 months

What now? From the early months of this loss, I've always had a mental list of things to do for Noah. I needed to feel active and continue to do things for him and his memory, just as I do things for or with my living son. There were people to contact, supports to seek out, books to read, memorials to arrange, blog entries to post, donations to make. I told friends about things I'd done for Noah's memory in the same way they caught me up on the latest news from their kids. These actions were a way to keep Noah's name and my grief part of daily conversation. It was comforting to still have him on my mental calendar, maybe because having things to do makes grievers feel purposeful and counteracts our sense of helplessness (Jeffreys, 2011).

Now as Bryan and I approach the three-year mark, there's less and less to do. Of course, there's still much to learn about suicide. Bryan and I are still mulling over a way to do good in the world in Noah's name, and I'm still keeping my blog and working on this book. I'm increasingly involved in the suicide loss support and suicide prevention communities. But these are mainly public tasks. The personal items on the list are diminishing as we have less contact with Noah's friends and fewer occasions to remember him.

I just checked off a long overdue item on the list. I finally framed a large self-portrait that Noah did in his first and only college drawing class. At the frame store, they asked if I wanted the type of fixative for the charcoal drawing that allows for further alterations; no, that wouldn't be necessary. This piece, like Noah, was finished forever, its imperfections suspended in time. There would be no more chances for Noah to master technique and refine his vision or for us to enjoy his accomplishments. All we'll ever have of his artistic aspirations are novice drawings and photographs.

We have the satisfaction now of living with Noah's pensive, larger-than-life face in our den. But we also have the emptiness of contemplating a shrinking to-do list. The list is the unfinished business of our connection to Noah, drawn out as long as possible. Its tasks are our efforts to say the goodbye that his suicide denied us. What now?

TO MY FELLOW SURVIVORS:
How are you managing the ups, numbs, and downs with the passing of time? How have your mood, spirit, and ability to cope been shifting since the suicide? Do you set aside time to tend to your grief—and time to restore your life—as you move through each phase?

Energizing and Expanding Your Breath

We tend to feel contracted and small when we're grieving, sunk into our sorrow in retreat from the world. The yoga practice of breath of fire can be a powerful tool for moving the energy, feeling expansive, and reconnecting with the flow.

First practice just the breath of fire: Breathing through your nose, begin inhaling and exhaling forcefully so you can hear it. Gradually quicken the pace so you are pumping your belly out (on the inhale) and in (on the exhale); place your hand over your navel to feel this. (You can see demonstrations of breath of fire on yoga websites or YouTube.) When you're comfortable, try the exercise:

- While sitting or standing, close your eyes, straighten your spine, and take a few deep cleansing breaths with your eyes closed.

- Raise your arms straight out to a 60-degree angle on either side of your head. Stick up your thumbs and curl your other fingers into a fist.

- Add breath of fire, the forceful intake and outtake through the nose. You should hear your breath and feel your belly pumping in and out.

- Speed up the breath of fire while holding the position. Keep the rest of the body relaxed.

- Do this for one minute at first, gradually building up to three minutes or more.

- To conclude, take a deep inhale and hold the breath as you bring your thumbs together above your head. Then slowly, on the exhale, bring your hands down to your heart in prayer position and breathe deeply in and out.

Adapted from Kundalini yoga practice

Chapter 14

"CLIMBING INTO THE DAY"

Reintegrating and Moving Forward

I did not know the work of mourning
Is like carrying a bag of cement
Up a mountain at night

The mountaintop is not in sight
Because there is no mountaintop
Poor Sisyphus grief…

Look closely and you will see
Almost everyone carrying bags
Of cement on their shoulders

That's why it takes courage
To get out of bed in the morning
And climb into the day.

Edward Hirsch (2014)

No Silver Linings but Maybe, Gifts—@ 6 months

It was my doctor who first warned me there's no silver lining. This was not meant to be and Noah is not in a better place. He's not resting in peace and we survivors are certainly not at peace with his death. There's no upside to this suffering. Even if there was, we'd reject it because we don't want to benefit in any way from our son's suicide.

More seasoned survivors talk about the "gifts" that this loss can bring. They do this to give themselves and the rest of us hope—no small thing. The gifts may not be easy to recognize at first, they say, but gifts will come and be part of your healing. I notice this in others though I can't yet see it for myself. I see that some survivors rebuild their lives to be more mindful and compassionate, with a more urgent sense of the preciousness of life. Through support groups, conferences, and crisis lines, they meet a new community of friends with whom they share an instant bond. Of necessity, they grasp for and find new reasons to live. Over time, they're grateful for the changes in their lives.

"The jury's still out," my husband, Bryan, says doubtfully. Six months after Noah's suicide, I'm not counting on any magical transformation or even counting my blessings. Yet I notice change.

Once someone who projected strength and confidence, I've been showing my vulnerability and sharing my feelings more openly with others, including strangers. With my blog, I have a vehicle to pour out my heart and recapture my love of writing. I've stumbled on support in unlikely places with fellow survivors, distant relatives, old friends I haven't spoken with in years.

These changes have happened as part of grief work. They'll never make up for the horror of Noah's death and the sinking sense of despair when I think of it. But they make sorrow a bit more bearable, the future more conceivable. And maybe they count as blessings.

Lightening the Burden—@ 19 months

For months, I've been haunted by an image of myself standing alone on a beach holding a long rope that's flung out to sea. Out past the horizon, the rope is attached to my dead son, twined around his torso. Noah floats in his beloved ocean, still tethered to me. He needs me to let go so he can float free. I hold on for fear that if I let go, he'll be lost to me forever. I hold on to be with him as mother-protector in a way that I couldn't while his life was ebbing. If I let go, I accept that he's truly dead and gone.

"Play with the rope," my therapist urges. "What if you let it out? What if you reel it in again? What are your options?" Extraordinary questions. I avoid thinking about them for a while and add more of my own.

The rope I envision is taut; there's no coil of excess at my feet. I'm at the end of my rope, as Noah was at the end of his. I'm holding on for dear life. The tide tugs; his body pulls. The rope he used for death I want to be a lifesaver—his and mine. The rope is my hope that I can always feel close to him and love him. I wasn't the kind of mother who could easily let go when he left home, so how can I possibly let go now?

Why rope as what binds me to Noah? The rope he used to kill himself lay on the floor as I hugged him for the last time. It was the last thing he touched. I'm holding onto the sight of his dead body, the unspeakable scene of his death, my guilt for not shielding him from his demons. It's those things I need to let go to leave him in peace and find my own. I need to say goodbye to my dead, despairing son so I can begin to remember him living and laughing. I feel lighter after saying this out loud in therapy.

The next day, my students and I are reading a children's book about lost tooth customs around the world, and I tell them a story about Noah at age six. The going rate in our house for the Tooth Fairy was 50 cents a tooth. Once after losing a tooth, Noah left a note under his pillow: *$2 or leave it!* My students laugh and I smile.

Uncommon Wisdom on Making Peace with Loss—@ 21 months

Common wisdom says you shouldn't make big decisions when grieving. But I need to make some changes in my work life in order to have time to grieve and write. I'm afraid of venturing into the unknown from this place of vulnerability, unsure whether my desire for change can be trusted. I'm not who I was and don't yet know who I'm becoming in the wake of this loss.

In the past few days, I received some uncommon wisdom from friends and fellow survivors. When I told my dear, oldest friend that I was afraid I'd see this decision about work differently later on, once I was more at peace with Noah's suicide, she said, "When you're more at peace, you'll be able to use that energy for the things you love and want to do. And if peace still eludes you at times, you'll have the space to do the grief work and other things for yourself that you're not able to do now." This is perfectly clear to my friend, though it's still murky to me; I thank her for showing me a way forward.

At a holiday gathering of survivors on the theme of making peace with our loss, I was struck by simple statements from people who lost loved ones eight or more years ago. From a woman who lost her sister: "I have made peace with no peace." From someone I can't recall: "Don't be afraid to remember." And from another mother who lost her young adult son, one word: "Endure." That's been her watchword for getting through the pain and for what she wants to happen with her child's memory. She wrote her son's name and "endure" on a tag attached to an origami crane as part of the closing activity at the gathering. We were told that cranes symbolize healing, happiness, and spiritual enlightenment in Japanese and Chinese tradition.

For my crane for Noah, I wrote a traditional Jewish saying and one of my own: "May your memory be for a blessing. And may all who loved you find that blessing." The crane and my wish now flutter on our patio.

Reclaiming My Birthday—@ 23 months

It's easy to downplay our own birthdays after losing someone to suicide. What is there to celebrate? How to switch from crying fit to party mode?

Many people remembered my birthday this year, and I'm grateful. They took special care to mark the day because they know how hard these two years have been and want to help ease me back into "normal" pleasures. There were little gifts in the mail and a surprise delivery of strawberries and flowers from the farmer's market. There were songs on my voicemail, a call from Ben, and shout-outs on Facebook. There was a massage and a dance performance to enjoy with my husband. I spent the day doing as I pleased when I pleased, determined not to spend it working or mourning.

I wasn't planning a party this year. But a local theater was putting on the musical, *Threepenny Opera*, which I grew up singing, and I wanted to share it with friends. I decided to organize a theater party, even if I might not feel ready. Everyone I invited came, rooting for me to be able to enjoy life again. Though it was stressful at times, I was glad to be surrounded with people who cared about me and understood my grief journey.

Making Decisions on Unsteady Ground—@ 23 months

I decided to cut back to working half-time. Since Noah's suicide, I've felt too pressed to commune with his spirit and honor my need for grief work, writing, and self-care. I've hated having to put those needs aside day after day to attend to other obligations. I'm fortunate to be able to work part-time, and friends who knew that wondered why I hesitated to make the change.

Decisions after suicide loss are especially hard, says the wise facilitator of my support group, because we've come to doubt the decisions we made about our loved one while they were alive. We're still haunted by what-ifs. The fateful decisions we made or failed to make are still imprinted on our mind, obscuring the way to new decisions. It's hard to trust our judgment or the ground under our feet. We've become the unreliable narrators of our own lives. We're scrambling to get our footing in a house without a foundation that we're slowly rebuilding, brick by brick.

Suicide loss "assaults the assumptive world of the mourner," writes psychologist John Jordan (2011). "The suicide brings into question all of the things that the bereaved individual took for granted about the identity of the deceased, the nature of their relationship with that individual, and the mourner's own identity" (p. 181). The mourner's ultimate task, Jordan suggests, is to construct a "coherent narrative" (p. 182) about the suicide that is compassionate and "bearable for the survivor" (p. 189).

From unsteady ground, I've decided to take time out for my narrative. I hope I'll come to trust that decision.

What I Want—@ 24 months

I'm back to making lists as the second anniversary of Noah's death approaches, like I did in the early months. Now: What I Want.

What I really want: while gazing out the window one day to see Noah walk up the driveway, whole and healthy, smile spreading, bearing gifts from his two years away, telling me he's sorry, he's back, he loves me.

I can't have that, so I focus on other things:

- I want to remember Noah always, healthy, happy, himself.

- I want to recover memories of his life till they outweigh those of his decline and death.

- I want to see him in my dreams.

- I want to feel his presence when I expect it, like at the ocean, and when I least expect it, anywhere, anytime.

- I want family and friends to share their memories and speak his name.

- I want to look at the star jasmine that blooms so sweetly in the yard and remember Noah's spirit with gladness, not bitterness.

- I want to spend more time with my son, Ben, and hold him close.

- I want to meet more mourning moms and talk, cry, and heal with them.

- I want to have all the time I need to grieve and write.

- I want to be open to the possibility of joy.

Of Culminations and Arrivals—@ 26 months

'Tis the late spring season of culminations and arrivals. I'm about to begin semi-retirement and open the way for other pursuits.

It seems fitting that in the seven weeks since Passover, I've been following a symbolic Jewish "journey of the soul" from slavery to freedom with the teachings of Rabbis Zimmerman and Enger (2015). They suggest seven stages, which are also evocative themes for the journey of grief after suicide as we try to recover our balance: Waking Up; Setting Out; Entering the Wilderness; Being in the Unknown; Finding Our Way; Becoming the Vision; and Arriving. I've spent a lot of time Entering the Wilderness and Being in the Unknown. I've gone in and out of Finding Our Way, still far from Vision or Arriving. What matters, I think, is being aware of Setting Out in the first place—with the intentional mourning and the willingness to talk openly about suicide and grief that researchers say are essential to healing (Dyregrov *et al.* 2012; Wolfelt 2009).

I'm still overcome with intense bouts of grief and guilt, but they're shorter now. Many mornings, I come awake bathed in long, sustaining breath and a sense of gratitude that I thought I'd never recover. I'm grateful that I knew and loved my lost child. I'm grateful for the support that got me through the worst of the pain. I'm grateful to be alive and healthy.

Next week brings another arrival as I take part in a group adult bat mitzvah celebration. With the momentousness of the occasion, with all those who are and are not present, there will be tears, shared and bittersweet. I can choose to focus on who's not there to give me their blessing—or I can be heartened by the blessing of all those who've helped carry me on this journey and who are cheering for me to have something to celebrate.

The two years of preparation for the bat mitzvah coincide with the two years of living without Noah. For much of the first year, I couldn't concentrate on learning and saw everything through the dark lens of loss. I stuck with the class because I dimly thought it might give me a stake in the future, beyond loss. That it has. I thank God and lots of people for, as the prayer says, allowing me to reach this season.

New Directions in the New Year—@ 30 months

Reading my list of intentions for the Jewish new year, I was appalled to see I made no mention of Noah. In the past, I always had a resolution for being my better self with each family member. This year, I thought about finding daily ways to remember Noah but forgot to put it on the list, much less anything about forgiveness. It was as if Noah had slipped from my consciousness. I joked with my support group that I'd have to atone for the omission. The facilitator said that Noah's absence from the list means I'm starting to focus on rebuilding.

When did I feel like my best self over the past year? When reaching out to other suicide loss survivors and creating experiences to help them move through grief, like the program of music to accompany grief that I helped organize for a survivors potluck. When using my voice to help others understand survivors' experience, like speaking on a panel on youth suicide. When leading singing, study, or meditation to enrich spiritual life in my Jewish community. Grief has propelled me into greater expression of caring, compassion, and creativity.

Therese Rando (1984) says that mourners must create a new relationship with the person they lost and a new identity for themselves. I can see an identity shift in progress, but I'm stuck when it comes to recreating my relationship with Noah. Maybe I'm still mourning the part of me that engaged with him and died with him.

"Thought after thought, feeling after feeling, action after action, had H. for their object," C.S. Lewis (2015 [1961], p.59) wrote after his wife's death. "Now their target is gone. I keep on through habit fitting an arrow to the string, then I remember and have to lay the bow down" (p. 59).

All the parts of me that were linked to Noah, involved in raising and loving him over the years and thinking about, worrying about, and reaching out to him as a young adult have been slowly leaching out of me since his suicide. It's wrenching. I don't know what can ever replace all those connections of love and care. How can a one-sided relationship to the past and to memory be a relationship at all?

Psychologist J. Shep Jeffreys (2011), who lost his eight-year-old son to cancer, writes eloquently of how bereaved parents might reconfigure their relationship to the dead child. "Over time, the parent reorganizes the inner picture of the lost child from one who was available in a real, physical sense to one who is available only in memory" and thoughts (p. 153). For parents and other bereaved people, this new connection can be seen as a "spiritual bond." It's heartening to think that recreating my connection to Noah is a spiritual act that takes place in my deepest being.

Ruminations on Post-Traumatic Growth—@ 34 months

Maybe you've heard about "post-traumatic growth" (PTG), the positive changes that psychologists say can arise from dealing with extreme adversity. I bring it up not as something to crow about or strive for—it doesn't work that way—but as something to offer light and hope to survivors and others facing traumatic events.

I didn't pay much attention early on when more seasoned survivors talked about PTG as a counterweight to post-traumatic stress. I was incredulous that anything good could come from this horror. I resisted the idea, not only because it felt so alien but because it seemed to belittle the tragedy of suicide. Harold Kushner (2004) writes in *When Bad Things Happen to Good People* that of course, if he could choose to have his teenage son back from illness rather than his own spiritual growth as a result of loss, he would, but he doesn't get that choice. We can't reverse the devastation that happened but inevitably, trauma changes us and if we're lucky, we can change in ways that help heal ourselves and the world.

Psychologists describe PTG as an ongoing transformative process that co-exists with distress about the traumatic event. The positive changes of PTG occur in five domains: our appreciation of life, the quality of our relationships, sense of our own strength, new life opportunities, and spirituality (Cann *et al.,* 2010;

Tedeschi & Calhoun, 2004). PTG arises not just from enduring the trauma but from the struggle to deal with the "earthquake" that shatters our core beliefs or "assumptive world" (Tedeschi & Calhoun, 2004, p.5). Oddly, the more resilient you are, the less likely you are to go through the "cognitive processing" (p. 9) of PTG. Instead, PTG comes from "rumination" (p. 9), going over and over what happened and your reaction to it as you try to make sense of it and reconstruct your schemas, or ways of seeing the world.

Experts distinguish between "brooding" rumination that is involuntary, depressive, and haunted by intrusive thoughts (like many of us have in the early stages of trauma) versus more reflective, "deliberate" rumination that actively seeks meaning (Tedeschi & Calhoun, 2004, p. 9). Jumping into problem-solving too quickly in search of closure can get in the way of PTG because "distress keeps the cognitive processing active" (p. 8). Other factors that promote PTG include expressing your emotions and telling your story in a supportive environment, like support groups.

What validation all this is for those of us who are inclined to think and talk about our loss rather than downplay our grief and quickly resume normal activities! PTG is part of the "new normal" we're trying so hard to construct and understand. It's an answer to the well-meaning folks who think there's no point continuing to ask why or process our feelings about the suicide. Learning about PTG reminds me how fortunate I've been to have access not only to support groups, therapy, and companions in grief, but to my journal, blog, and this book as vehicles for rumination—and readers who respond in such encouraging ways to my wandering thoughts. Thanks to all of you for being part of my cognitive processing!

There are no guarantees. PTG will remain elusive for some and of little interest to others. But its occurrence is significant and what survivor and social worker Lisa Richards (2014) calls "a powerful silver lining for us grievers."

(You can read about suicide loss survivors of diverse backgrounds, personalities, and circumstances who became more loving, generous people after their loss, including becoming suicide prevention activists, mental health advocates, healers, researchers, and artists, in Jordan and Baugher [2016], Bolton [2017], and other Recommended Resources at the back of this book).

Opening My House: Remembering Noah @ 25—@ 36 months

There's no conclusion to a book about suicide loss, no culminating summit for mourners bearing their grief up the mountain, as poet Edward Hirsch (2014) says. Each person who walks the mourner's path after suicide leaves their own unique footprint. If we're lucky, we meet others and follow their tracks or walk beside them, discovering more pathways and vistas for ourselves and others as we climb.

The old women in a Greek village who schooled me in mourning years ago had good advice after I lost my parents. They knew I was an orphan without spouse or siblings. "Go back to America," they said, "and open your house." I offer the same advice to my fellow survivors of suicide loss: At some point, even if you're not completely ready, open your house. Reconnect with life and the people you love.

For what would have been Noah's 25th birthday this June, we'll open our house for a celebration of his life. Some use that term for funerals and memorials, but it's impossible to celebrate right after a suicide. Now after more than three years, we feel ready to remember and appreciate the sweep of Noah's life in community with the people who loved him.

Bryan and I are gladdened at the prospect of seeing Noah's friends, relatives, and French host family all gathered in one place before more time goes by, paths diverge, and memories fade. One of Noah's gifts was bringing people together. In honoring that gift on this occasion, we hope to bring healing to our family and to the many people who miss Noah. For me, who used to love organizing celebrations, this could be a new beginning after so much mourning.

We're planning a table full of Noah's favorite foods, like sushi, peanut butter pretzels, and Kinder Bueno candies. We'll have another table with a slideshow, scrapbooks, and mementos like Noah's tiny water polo team Speedo swimsuit and a list he made of his favorite independent films. There will be time to share memories both familiar and new…something to look forward to!

With this event, Bryan and I remind ourselves of the lives we are restoring. As we open our house, we open our hearts.

TO MY FELLOW SURVIVORS:

What signs of growth have you noticed in the wake of trauma? Give yourself credit for every step forward, no matter how small. Wishing you something to look forward to as you move through your grief and open your house. I share your sorrow. I share your hope.

Dancing in the Kitchen

Grief lodges in the body. Give yourself a chance to move the energy that's blocked by pain. Find a place where you feel free to move. (For me, this is alone in my kitchen.) Put on some infectious music that fills your body and makes you feel like dancing. Let go, be wild, dance like you've never danced before—because you're not who you were before. Shake it up, cry it out, get breathless. Who says you can't mourn and dance at the same time? Let it out. Revitalize the life force that will carry you forward as you "climb into the day."

Noah preparing to climb Half Dome, Yosemite National Park, 2010.

BEYOND SURVIVING: SUGGESTIONS FOR SURVIVORS BY IRIS M. BOLTON

1. Know you can survive. You may not think so, but you can.

2. Struggle with "why" it happened until you no longer need to know "why" or until YOU are satisfied with partial answers.

3. Know you may feel overwhelmed by the intensity of your feelings but that all your feelings are normal.

4. Anger, guilt, confusion, forgetfulness are common responses. You are not crazy; you are in mourning.

5. Be aware you may feel appropriate anger at the person, at the world, at God, at yourself. It's okay to express it.

6. You may feel guilty for what you think you did or did not do. Guilt can turn into regret, through forgiveness.

7. Having suicidal thoughts is common. It does not mean that you will act on those thoughts.

8. Remember to take one moment or one day at a time.

9. Find a good listener with whom to share. Call someone if you need to talk.

10. Don't be afraid to cry. Tears are healing.

11. Give yourself time to heal.

12. Remember, the choice was not yours. No one is the sole influence in another's life.

13. Expect setbacks. If emotions return like a tidal wave, you may only be experiencing a remnant of grief, an unfinished piece.

14. Try to put off major decisions.

15. Give yourself permission to get professional help.

16. Be aware of the pain of your family and friends.

17. Be patient with yourself and with others who may not understand.

18. Set your own limits and learn to say no.

19. Steer clear of people who want to tell you *what* or *how* to feel.

20. Know that there are support groups that can be helpful, such as Compassionate Friends or Survivors of Suicide groups. If not, ask a professional to help start one.

21. Call on your personal faith to help you through.

22. It is common to experience physical reaction to your grief, e.g. headaches, loss of appetite, inability to sleep.

23. The willingness to laugh with others and at yourself is healing.

24. Wear out your questions, anger, guilt, or other feelings until you can let them go. Letting go doesn't mean forgetting.

25. Know that you will never be the same again, but you can survive and even go beyond just surviving.

REFERENCES

Anderson, S. (2008, July 6). The urge to end it all. *New York Times Magazine.* Accessed on 9/2/2017 at www.nytimes.com/2008/07/06/magazine/06suicide-t.html?pagewanted=all

Antus, M. (2013, January 23). Suicide bereavement and forgiveness [Web log post]. Accessed on 9/2/2017 at http://marysshortcut.com/2013/01/23/suicide-bereavement-and-forgiveness/

Bialosky, J. (2011). *History of a suicide: My sister's unfinished life.* New York: Washington Square Press.

Bolton, I. (1983). *My son... my son...: A guide to healing after death, loss, or suicide.* Roswell, GA: Bolton Press.

Bolton, I. (1987). Beyond surviving: Suggestions for survivors. In E.J. Dunne, J.L. McIntosh, and K. Dunne-Maxim (Eds), *Suicide and its aftermath: Understanding and counseling the survivors* (pp. 289–290). New York: Norton.

Bonny, D. (2015, April 21). Unraveling the aftermath of suicide loss: Healing those left behind [tele-conference]. (See also Bonny's website www.livingonthefaultlines.com).

Brener, A. (2012). *Mourning and mitzvah: A guided journal for walking the mourner's path through grief to healing* (2nd ed.). Woodstock, VT: Jewish Lights Publishing.

Cann, A., Calhoun, L.G., Tedeschi, R.G., Taku, K. *et al.* (2010). A short form of the Posttraumatic Growth Inventory. *Anxiety, Stress &Coping, 23*(2), 127–137. Accessed on 28/2/2017 at https://ptgi.uncc.edu/wp-content/uploads/sites/9/2015/01/A-short-form-of-the-Posttraumatic-Growth-Inventory.pdf

Collins, D. (compiler) (n.d.). A bereaved parent's wish list. Accessed on 9/2/2017 at www.thecompassionatefriend.org/links&articles.htm#Bereaved

Comins, M. (2007). *A wild faith: Jewish ways into wilderness, wilderness ways into Judaism.* Woodstock, VT: Jewish Lights Publishing.

Comins, M. (2010). *Making prayer real: Leading Jewish spiritual voices on why prayer is difficult and what to do about it*. Woodstock, VT: Jewish Lights Publishing.

Cook, J. (2010, April). Living in new skin. *Grief Digest Magazine, 7*(14), 18–19. Accessed on 28/2/2017 at www.griefdigestmagazine.com/magazine-articles/article/2017/02/20/living-in-new-skin

Cook, J. (2013, December 29). "Happy?" new year [Web log post]. Accessed on 9/2/2017 at http://livingwiththelossofachild.blogspot.com/2013/12/happy-new-year.html

Cook, J. (2014, February 6). The power of the pause [Web log post]. Accessed on 9/2/2017 at http://livingwiththelossofachild.blogspot.com/2014/02/the-power-of-pause.html

Dyregrov, K., Plyhn, E., & Dieserud, G. (2012). *After the suicide: Helping the bereaved to find a path from grief to recovery*. Translated by Diane Oatley. Philadelphia, PA: Jessica Kingsley Publishers.

Erskine, C. (2014, November 27). A relic unearthed: The black-and-white holiday family photo. *Los Angeles Times*. Accessed on 9/2/2017 at www.latimes.com/home/la-hm-erskine-20141129-column.html

essence & Pease, J. (2009). Shape of you [song lyrics]. Jeffrey Pease Music (ASCAP).

Feigelman, W. (2008, October). The stigma of suicide and how it affects survivors' healing. *IASP Postvention Taskforce Newsletter, 12*(5). Accessed on 9/2/2017 at http://www3.ncc.edu/faculty/soc/feigelb/stigmashorterversion.pdf

Freedenthal, S. (2014, May 7). If only: Self-blame after a loved one's suicide [Web log post]. Accessed on 9/2/2017 at www.speakingofsuicide.com/2014/05/07/if-only/#sthash.SJH4UiIq.dpuf

Fumia, M. (2012). *Safe passage: Words to help the grieving*. San Francisco, CA: Conari Press.

Greenleaf, C. (2006). *Healing the hurt spirit: Daily affirmations for people who have lost a loved one to suicide*. Andover, NH: St. Dymphna Press.

Gutin, N.J., McGann, V., and Jordan, J. (2011). The impact of suicide on professional caregivers. In J. Jordan and J. McIntosh (Eds.), *Grief after suicide: Understanding the consequences and caring for the survivors* (pp. 93–114). New York: Routledge.

Hecht, J.M. (2010, February 7). Stay. *Boston Globe*. Accessed on 9/2/2017 at www.boston.com/bostonglobe/ideas/articles/2010/02/07/stay/

Hecht, J.M. (2013). *Stay: A history of suicide and the arguments against it*. New Haven, CT: Yale University Press.

Heckler, R. (n.d.). The suicidal trance. Alliance of Hope for Suicide Loss Survivors. Accessed on 9/2/2017 at www.allianceofhope.org/survivor_experience/richard-heckler-on-the-suicidal-trance.html

Hirsch, E. (2014). *Gabriel: A poem*. New York: Knopf.

Jamison, K.R. (1999). *Night falls fast: Understanding suicide.* New York: Vintage.

Jeffreys, J.S. (2011). *Helping grieving people – when tears are not enough: A handbook for care providers* (2nd ed.). New York: Routledge.

Joiner, T. (2005). *Why people die by suicide.* Cambridge, MA: Harvard University Press.

Jordan, J. (2011). Principles of grief counseling with adult survivors. In J. Jordan and J. McIntosh (Eds.), *Grief after suicide: Understanding the consequences and caring for the survivors* (pp. 179–224). New York: Routledge.

Jordan, J. & Baugher, B. (2016). *After the suicide: Coping with your grief* (2nd ed.). Newcastle, WA: Caring People Press.

Kedar, K. (2007). *The bridge to forgiveness: Stories and prayers for finding God and restoring wholeness.* Woodstock, VT: Jewish Lights Publishing.

Keltner, D. & Ekman, P. (2015, July 3). The science of 'Inside Out.' *New York Times.* Accessed on 9/2/2017 at www.nytimes.com/2015/07/05/opinion/sunday/the-science-of-inside-out.html?_r=0

Klay, P. (2014, February 9). After war, a failure of the imagination. *New York Times,* SR 4.

Kushner, H.S. (2004). *When bad things happen to good people.* New York: Anchor Books.

Lasseter, J. (Producer), and Docter, P. & Del Carmen, R. (Directors) (2015). *Inside Out* [motion picture]. US: Pixar Animation Studios.

Leenaars, A.A. (2010). Review: Edwin S. Shneidman on suicide. *Suicidology Online, 1,* 5–18.

Lesoine, R.E. & Chöphel, M. (2013). *Unfinished conversation: Healing from suicide and loss. A guided journey.* Berkeley, CA: Parallax Press.

Levy, Y. (2013, November 18). "When it's hard to say 'I'm thankful' on Thanksgiving." *Huffington Post.* Accessed on 9/2/2017 at www.huffingtonpost.com/rabbi-yael-levy/when-its-hard-to-say-im-t_b_4276738.html?utm_hp_ref=email_share

Lewis, C.S. (2015 [1961]). *A grief observed.* New York: HarperOne.

Lindbergh, A.M. (1993 [1973]). *Hour of gold, hour of lead: Diaries and letters of Anne Morrow Lindbergh 1929–1932.* New York: Mariner Books.

Macdonald, H. (2014). *H is for hawk.* New York: Grove Press.

MacFarquhar, L. (2013, June 24). Last call: A Buddhist monk confronts Japan's suicide culture. *The New Yorker.*

McLachlan, S., Egan, S., & Merenda, D. (1995). *I will remember you* [song lyrics]. T C F Music Publishing, Inc. (ASCAP), Seamus Egan Music, Sony/ATV Songs LLC., Tyde Music (BMI).

Mason, W. (2014, October 1). The revelations of Marilynne Robinson. *New York Times Magazine.* Accessed on 9/2/2017 at www.nytimes.com/2014/10/05/magazine/the-revelations-of-marilynne-robinson.html?_r=1

Maya, C. (2014, February 25). Deathaversary [Web log post]. Accessed on 9/2/2017 at www.sushituesdays.com

Milton, J.P. (2006). *Sky above, earth below: Spiritual practices in nature.* Boulder, CO: Sentient Publications.

NAMI (National Alliance on Mental Illness) and Jed Foundation. (2016). *Starting the conversation: College and your mental health.* Accessed on 9/2/2017 at www.nami.org/collegeguide/download

Neff, K. (2015). Self-compassion meditation. Accessed on 9/2/2017 at http://self-compassion.org/wp-content/uploads/2015/12/self-compassion.break_.mp3

O'Rourke, M. (2011). *The long goodbye: A memoir.* New York: Riverhead Books.

O'Rourke, M. (2015, April 26). To have loved and lost. *New York Times Book Review,* 16.

Rabbinical Assembly (1998). Yizkor memorial service: A personal meditation. In *Siddur Sim Shalom for Shabbat and festivals.* New York: Rabbinical Assembly, The United Synagogue of Conservative Judaism.

Rando, T.A. (1984). *Grief, dying, and death: Clinical interventions for caregivers.* Champaign, IL: Research Press.

Rando, T.A. (1993). *Treatment of complicated mourning.* Champaign, IL: Research Press.

Richards, L. (2012). *Dear Mallory: Letters to a teenage girl who killed herself.* Torrance, CA: New Middle Press.

Richards, L. (2014, February 7). Trauma as strength training? Yep [Web log post]. Accessed on 9/2/2017 at https://griefsnewleaf.wordpress.com/2014/02/07/trauma-as-strength-training-yep/

Schneider, J. (1994). *Finding my way: Healing and transformation through loss and grief.* Colfax, WI: Seasons Press.

Shneidman, E.S. (2008). *A commonsense book of death: Reflections at ninety of a lifelong thanatologist.* Lanham, MD: Rowman & Littlefield.

Silverman, J. (2013, May 31). The artful meditation of Karen Green, David Foster Wallace's widow. *Los Angeles Times.* Accessed on 28/2/2017 at http://articles.latimes.com/2013/may/31/entertainment/la-ca-jc-karen-green-david-foster-wallace-20130602

Solomon, A. (2014, August 14). Suicide, a crime of loneliness. *The New Yorker.* Accessed on 9/2/2017 at www.newyorker.com/culture/cultural-comment/suicide-crime-loneliness

Strouse, S. (2013). *Artful grief: A diary of healing.* Bloomington, IN: Balboa Press.

Tedeschi, R.G. & Calhoun, L.G. (2004). Posttraumatic growth: Conceptual foundations and empirical evidence. *Psychological Inquiry, 15*(1), 1–18.

Telushkin, J. (1991). *Jewish literacy: The most important things to know about the Jewish religion, its people, and its history.* New York: William Morrow and Co.

Walker, R. (2014, July 1). Is suicide 100% preventable? Probably not… Alliance of Hope for Suicide Loss Survivors. Accessed on 9/2/2017 at www.allianceofhope.org/blog_/2014/07/page/2/

Wickersham, J. (2008). *The suicide index: Putting my father's death in order.* Orlando, FL: Harcourt.

Wolfelt, A.D. (2009). *Understanding your suicide grief: Ten essential touchstones for finding hope and healing your heart.* Fort Collins, CO: Companion Press.

Wordsworth, W. (1800). Preface to Lyrical Ballads. *Famous Prefaces: The Harvard Classics, 1909–14.* Accessed on 9/2/2017 at www.bartleby.com/39/36.html

Zimmerman, J. (2015, November 10). *Hineni:* The mindful heart community [teleconference]. Accessed on 9/2/2017 at www.ravjill.com/hineni-the-mindful-heart-community/

Zimmerman, J. and Enger, C. (2015). Journey of the soul: Making the Omer count. Accessed on 9/2/2017 at www.ravjill.com/the-jewish-mindfulness-network/test-omer/

Zulli, A. (2014, March/April). Choosing life. *Beyond Loss* newsletter. Glendale, CA: Glendale Adventist Hospital Beyond Loss Bereavement Ministry.

RECOMMENDED RESOURCES ON SUICIDE AND SUICIDE LOSS: A SAMPLING

If you or someone you know are thinking about suicide, please contact one of the suicide prevention hotlines below:

In the US, call National Suicide Prevention Hotline 1-800-273-8255 (or text START to 741-741).

In the UK, call Samaritans 08457 90 90 90 or 116 123 or HopeLine UK 0800 068 414.

In Canada, see http://suicideprevention.ca/need-help for provincial hotlines.

In Australia, call Lifeline Australia 13 11 14.

In other countries, see www.iasp.info/resources/Crisis_Centres.

If you are in immediate danger, call emergency services or go to the nearest emergency room.

Below is a short, partial list of recommended resources. For many more excellent resources, see the listings in the books and websites below, especially the websites of the American Association of Suicidology and the American Foundation for Suicide Prevention.

Understanding and Preventing Suicide
Selected Books and Articles

Ferris, A. (Ed.) (2015). *Shades of blue: Writers on depression, suicide, and feeling blue.* Berkeley, CA: Seal Press. (Short personal essays that provide perspective and encouragement to people who are struggling, as well as understanding to those who wish to help.)

Hecht, J.M. (2013). *Stay: A history of suicide and the arguments against it.* New Haven, CT: Yale University Press. (Review of Western philosophical and religious views on suicide that culminates in impassioned plea to those in distress to "stay.")

Jamison, K.R. (1999). *Night falls fast: Understanding suicide.* New York: Vintage. (Classic account of suicidality by a psychiatrist who lives with bipolar disorder and has a history of suicide attempts; emphasizes the mental illness explanation.)

Joiner, T. (2005). *Why people die by suicide.* Cambridge, MA: Harvard University Press. (A research psychologist's three-part theory of suicide based on the thwarting of the need to connect and the need to contribute, combined with an acquired ability to self-harm.)

Joiner, T. (2010). *Myths about suicide.* Cambridge, MA: Harvard University Press. (Draws on his earlier book to address common misunderstandings about suicide.)

Leenaars, A.A. (2010). Review: Edwin S. Shneidman on suicide. *Suicidology Online, 1,* 5–18. (Succinct review of Shneidman's pioneering work in suicidology.)

Shneidman, E.S. (1995). *Suicide as psychache: A clinical approach to suicidal behavior.* Lanham, MD: Rowman & Littlefield. (One of the later works of renowned suicidologist Edwin Shneidman.)

Solomon, A. (2001). *The noonday demon: An atlas of depression.* New York: Simon & Schuster. (Detailed account of the author's lifelong struggle with depression; also documents a wide variety of others' experience with the disorder.)

Selected Websites

American Association of Suicidology (AAS) www.suicidology.org

Information on suicide and suicide prevention, professional training opportunities, publications, and annual research conference.

American Foundation for Suicide Prevention (AFSP) https://afsp.org

Information on suicide and suicide prevention, with emphasis on public awareness, advocacy, fundraising, and volunteering.

Australian Suicide Prevention Foundation (ASPF) http://suicideprevention.com.au

Information and resources on suicide risk and prevention.

Canadian Association for Suicide Prevention (CASP) http://suicideprevention.ca/

Information and resources on understanding, preventing, and coping with suicide.

International Association for Suicide Prevention (IASP) www.iasp.info

International resources on suicide prevention and postvention, as well as IASP publications and information on annual conference, special interest groups, and World Suicide Prevention Day.

Jed Foundation www.jedfoundation.org

Resources and training for parents, college students, and college professionals to promote emotional health and prevent suicide among college students.

Man Therapy www.mantherapy.org

Unique, interactive website that uses humor and quirky graphics to promote help-seeking, mental health, and suicide prevention among men; a project of the Colorado Office of Suicide Prevention and the Carson J. Spencer Foundation. A new take on "manning up"!

National Organization for People of Color Against Suicide http://nopcas.org/

Information, resources, and connections around suicide prevention and support by and for people of color.

Samaritans www.samaritans.org

Well-established organization in the UK that promotes mental health and suicide prevention through crisis centers, training, and other services.

Speaking of Suicide www.speakingofsuicide.com

Compassionate, authoritative blog entries on wide variety of suicide-related topics for suicidal people, as well as friends and family, survivors, and clinicians by Dr. Stacey Freedenthal, a psychotherapist and researcher who specializes in crisis intervention and suicide prevention.

Suicide Prevention Resource Center www.sprc.org

Promotes best practices in suicide prevention with public health approach through training and advocacy with professionals, institutions, nonprofits, and US government agencies.

ULifeline www.ulifeline.org

> Appealing resource on emotional and mental health aimed at American college students, with helpful background information on mental illness and suicide, self-evaluator tool, tips on helping friends in crisis, personal stories, etc. A project of the JED Foundation.

Understanding and Coping with Suicide Loss
Selected Books and Articles

Antus, M. (2014). *My daughter, her suicide, and God: A memoir of hope.* CreateSpace (Amazon). (Compassionately explores a teenage girl's suicide and its impact on the author's family, faith, and spiritual life.)

Bialosky, J. (2011). *History of a suicide: My sister's unfinished life.* New York: Washington Square Press. (Memoir in poetry and prose, placing the author's younger sister's suicide in the context of family dynamics and the author's other losses, as well as views on suicide from psychology and literature.)

Biancolli, A. (2014). *Figuring sh!t out: Love, laughter, suicide, and survival.* Burlington, IA: Behler Publications. (Brings remarkable humor and resilience to the story of how the author and her children coped and thrived after the author's husband's suicide. See also related blog.)

Bolton, I. (1983). *My son...my son...: A guide to healing after death, loss, or suicide.* Roswell, GA: Bolton Press. (Wise, trailblazing account of suicide loss by one of the founders of the survivors support movement.)

Bolton, I. (2017). *Voices of healing and hope: Conversations on grief after suicide.* Atlanta, GA: Bolton Press. (Book and DVD available from www.irisbolton.com based on interviews with survivors about eight key issues in suicide grief, such as guilt, anger, shame, and faith.)

Dyregrov, K., Plyhn, E., & Dieserud, G. (2012). *After the suicide: Helping the bereaved find a path from grief to recovery.* Translated by Diane Oatley. Philadelphia, PA: Jessica Kingsley Publications. (Helpful mix of personal narratives and research findings, based on a Norwegian study of suicide loss survivors.)

Feigelman, W., Jordan, J.R., McIntosh, J.L., & Feigelman, B. (2012). *Devastating losses: How parents cope with the loss of a child to suicide or drugs.* New York: Springer Publishing. (Report on a sociological study of over 500 parents in suicide survivors support groups.)

Fine, C. (1997). *No time to say goodbye: Surviving the suicide of a loved one.* New York: Broadway Books. (Artfully interweaves the author's experience of losing her husband to suicide with the stories of other suicide survivors she interviewed; much attention to issues of stigma, secrecy, and shame around suicide.)

Greenleaf, C. (2006). *Healing the hurt spirit: Daily affirmations for people who have lost a loved one to suicide.* Andover, NH: St. Dymphna Press. (Short, heartfelt affirmations for every day of the year that speak to many survivor concerns. See the author's blog at www.healingthehurtspirit. blogspot.com)

Jordan, J. (2011). Principles of grief counseling with adult survivors. In J. Jordan & J. McIntosh (Eds.), *Grief after suicide: Understanding the consequences and caring for the survivors* (pp. 179–224). New York: Routledge. (Useful for those seeking more in-depth psychological explanations of, as well as therapeutic approaches to, suicide grief by a top authority in the field.)

Jordan, J. & Baugher, B. (2016). *After the suicide: Coping with your grief* (2nd ed.). Newcastle, WA: Caring People Press. (Short, helpful guide to the suicide grief process by psychologists who specialize in suicide bereavement. New edition includes essays by a diverse group of survivors that attest to how they lived through and learned from the experience.)

Lesoine, R.E. & Chöphel, M. (2013). *Unfinished conversation: Healing from suicide and loss. A guided journey.* Berkeley, CA: Parallax Press. (Excellent suggestions for journaling, interactive dialogues, and meditation interwoven with memoir about losing a best friend to suicide. See also: Websites.)

Myers, M.F. & Fine, C. (2006). *Touched by suicide: Hope and healing after loss.* New York: Gotham Books. (Practical tips for survivors by a psychiatrist who specializes in suicide and survivor author Carla Fine.)

Richards, L. (2012). *Dear Mallory: Letters to a teenage girl who killed herself.* Torrance, CA: New Middle Press. (Loving letters from a therapist mother to Mallory, interweaving family memories with stages of the grief process.)

Strouse, S. (2013). *Artful grief: A diary of healing.* Bloomington, IN: Balboa Press. (Suicide loss memoir by an art therapist who used the art of collage to express and explore her grief for her daughter. See Strouse's collages at www.attherefuge.com under Photo Gallery.)

Wickersham, J. (2008). *The suicide index: Putting my father's death in order.* Orlando, FL: Harcourt. (Literary suicide loss memoir that paints an absorbing portrait of a father and family, while struggling with questions.)

Wolfelt, A.D. (2009). *Understanding your suicide grief: Ten essential touchstones for finding hope and healing your heart.* Fort Collins, CO: Companion Press. (Short, encouraging guide to dealing with stages of the suicide grief process by a psychologist specializing in bereavement.)

See also listings and reviews of books for survivors at AFSP http:// afsp.org/find-support/ive-lost-someone/resources-loss-survivors/ books-loss-survivors/ and AAS www.suicidology.org/resources/ recommended-reading#General%20Texts

Selected Websites

Alliance of Hope for Suicide Loss Survivors www.allianceofhope.org

> Information for survivors and free moderated online community forum, divided into useful topics related to suicide loss.

American Association of Suicidology (AAS) www.suicidology.org/suicide-survivors

> Information and resources for survivors, including directory of support groups in the U.S.

American Foundation for Suicide Prevention (AFSP) https://afsp.org/find-support/ive-lost-someone/

> Section for survivors includes support group listings, financial advice, books on suicide loss, Survivor Day video documentaries, etc.

Clinician Survivor Task Force, American Assn. of Suicidology www.cliniciansurvivor.org

> Information and support for clinicians and other professional caregivers who have lost patients/clients to suicide.

Unfinished Conversation www.unfinishedconversation.com

> Site for Lesoine's book listed above has many useful resources and updated links to news on suicide and suicide loss, plus "Toolkit for Your Journey to Healing."

> For support groups, services, and information for survivors in the UK, Australia, and Canada, see the following:

Suicide Bereavement Support Partnership www.supportaftersuicide.org.uk

Survivors of Bereavement by Suicide www.uk-sobs.org.uk

Postvention Australia: National Association for the Bereaved by Suicide www.postventionaustralia.org

Support After Suicide-Australia www.supportaftersuicide.org.au

Canadian Association for Suicide Prevention http://suicideprevention.ca/coping-with-suicide-loss/survivor-support-centres/

IASP's list of survivor organizations by country at www.iasp.info/resources/Postvention/National_Suicide_Survivor_Organizations/

> Please visit my blog, Walking the Mourner's Path After a Child's Suicide at http://afterachildssuicide.blogspot.com or my website, www.susanauerbachwriter.com for more information and resources. You're welcome to leave comments on the site or blog or to contact me privately at susanauerbach56@gmail.com

PERMISSIONS

Chapters 1, 9, and 13, song lyrics from essence and Jeffrey Pease (2009). Shape of you [song lyrics]. Jeffrey Pease Music (ASCAP).

Chapter 2, Zulli quote reproduced with permission from Zulli, A. (2014, March/April). Choosing life. *Beyond Loss* newsletter. Glendale, CA: Glendale Adventist Hospital Beyond Loss Bereavement Ministry.

Chapters 3 and 9, Wolfelt quotes reproduced with permission from Wolfelt, A.D. (2009). *Understanding your suicide grief: Ten essential touchstones for finding hope and healing your heart.* Fort Collins, CO: Companion Press.

Chapter 4, Wickersham quote reproduced with permission from Wickersham, J. (2008). *The suicide index: Putting my father's death in order.* Orlando, FL: Harcourt.

Chapter 5, Greenleaf quote reproduced with permission from Greenleaf, C. (2006). *Healing the hurt spirit: Daily affirmations for people who have lost a loved one to suicide.* Andover, NH: St. Dymphna Press.

Chapter 6, Bolton quote reproduced with permission from Bolton, I. (1983). *My son...my son...: A guide to healing after death, loss, or suicide.* Rowell, CA: Bolton Press.

Chapter 6, Freedenthal extract reproduced with permission from Freedenthal, S. (2014, May 7). If only: Self-blame after a loved one's suicide [Web log post].

Chapter 7, O'Rourke quote reproduced with permission from O'Rourke, M. (2011). *The long goodbye: A memoir.* New York: Riverhead Books.

Chapter 7, Levy extract reproduced with permission from Levy, Y. (2013, November 18). When it's hard to say "I'm thankful" on Thanksgiving. *Huffington Post.*

Chapter 8, Rabbinical Assembly quote reproduced with permission from Rabbinical Assembly (1998). Yizkor memorial service: A personal meditation. In *Siddur Sim Shalom for Shabbat and festivals*. New York: Rabbinical Assembly, The United Synagogue of Conservative Judaism.

Chapter 9, song lyrics from "I Will Remember You" written by Sarah McLachlan, Seamus Egan, and Dave Merenda © 1995 T C F Music Publishing, Inc. (ASCAP), Seamus Egan Music, Sony/ATV Songs LLC., Tyde Music (BMI). All Rights Reserved. Used by permission.

Chapter 10, Bonny quote reproduced with permission from Bonny, D. (2015, April 21). Unraveling the aftermath of suicide loss: Healing those left behind [tele-conference].

Chapter 11, Kedar quote reproduced with permission from Kedar, K. (2007). *The bridge to forgiveness: Stories and prayers for finding God and restoring wholeness*. Woodstock, VT: Jewish Lights Publishing.

Chapter 12, Shneidman quote reproduced with permission from Shneidman, E.S. (2008). *A commonsense book of death: Reflections at ninety of a lifelong thanatologist*. Lanham, MD: Rowman & Littlefield.

Chapter 13, Cook quote reproduced with permission from Cook, J. (2010, April). Living in new skin. *Grief Digest Magazine, 7*(14), 18–19.

Chapter 14, Hirsch quote reproduced with permission of Hirsch, E. (2014). *Gabriel: A poem*. New York: Knopf.

Appendix, 'Beyond Surviving: Suggestions for Survivors' by Iris Bolton. Reprinted with permission from Dunne, E.J., McIntosh, J.L., & Dunne-Maxim, K. (Eds.) (1987). *Suicide and its aftermath: Understanding and counseling the survivors* (pp. 289–290). New York: Norton.